STIRRING THE DEEP

The Poetry of Mark Vinz

Edited by Thom Tammaro

Spoon River Poetry Press
1989

"The Journey and the Return: The Poetry of Mark Vinz" appeared in a slightly different form in MINNESOTA REVIEWS, December, 1984. Vol. 2, #10. My thanks to the editors and Joanne Hart for inviting me to write the original essay.

Special thanks to Moorhead State University for providing an Excellence in Research Grant to support the completion of the manuscript.

This book is published in part with funds provided by the Illinois Arts Council, a state organization, and by the National Endowment for the Arts. Our thanks.

Grateful acknowledgement is made to all the editors who first published the poems in this manuscript. The Acknowledgements section at the end of this book constitutes the official acknowledgements page.

Published by:
Spoon River Poetry Press
David Pichaske, editor
P.O. Box 1443
Peoria, Illinois 61655

Typesetting:
BY ALL MEANS
1051 Virginia St.
St. Paul, MN 55117
The editor and publisher would like to thank Rob Schanilec of BY ALL MEANS for his deep interest and assistance in this project. The editor would also like to thank Sheila Coghill, Betsy Vinz, and Katie Vinz for their assistance preparing the final manuscript.

ISBN: 0-944024-18-1

Printing by: M & D Printing, Henry, Illinois

Spoon River Poetry Press
P.O. Box 1443
Peoria, Illinois 61655

CONTENTS

"Observe perpetually…"

— Henry James

"I wanted to write a poem
that you would understand.
For what good is it to me
if you can't understand it?
                    But you got to try hard—"

— William Carlos Williams

ARCHITECT OF POETRY

In his discussion of religious architecture, the great art historian Albert Elsen remarks that "the fact that we do not know the names of many of the architects who worked on the Gothic cathedrals—such as the principal one at Chartres—does not substantiate the view that they were anonymous in their own time" (*Purposes of Art,* 2nd ed. [NY: Holt, Rinehart, and Winston, Inc., 1967], p. 72). In many ways, the career and work of Mark Vinz—and others like him—share a similar fate in the world of contemporary poetry. Twenty-five years after offset printing revolutionized small press publishing in America and ushered in such mainstays of the literary world as the small, non-commercial literary press and magazine, literary distribution services, and such related activities as the poetry or fiction reading and—to a peripheral extent—writers-in-the-schools programs, the architects of the small press world remain virtually unknown except among the architects themselves. Like the worshipers found in the great European cathedrals, who need not know—or care—who the architects were in order to worship there, thousands of readers, writers, and students are active participants in the cathedral of contemporary poetry without knowing the names of the architects who designed the edifice.

Of the architects of contemporary poetry in the upper Midwest, Mark Vinz must be counted among them. Since the late 1960s, his work in small press is a record of tireless devotion. A brief account of his involvement with small press will illustrate, I believe, his commitment and dedication to the life of poetry and literature in the upper Midwest for nearly two decades. That alone is reason enough for this book which—like others in the series to follow—is designed to chronicle and celebrate those Midwestern writers, editors, and publishers—those sometimes unsung anonymous architects—who have contributed substantially to the literary and cultural life of the region.

To begin with, there is Vinz's work from 1971-81 as editor of the magazine, *Dacotah Territory* and its book publishing imprint Territorial Press—the full history of which has been written by Vinz himself in "Looking Back on Ten Years of *Dacotah Territory,*" published in *Dacotah Territory: A Ten Year Anthology* (ed. Vinz and Ray, Fargo, ND: North Dakota Institute for Regional Studies, 1982). During those ten years, over 16,000 copies of 17 issues of the magazine as well as over 7,000 copies of 15 books and chapbooks were published and distributed. The ten year life of the magazine itself gives testimony to the vitality of Vinz and Grayce Ray's (who joined Vinz as associate editor beginning with issue #4) vision—given the fact that the average life span of most literary magazines is less than five years—less than one-half of *Dacotah Territory*'s. But the content of the magazine is what is impressive. In this regard, I think of the many Midwestern writers whose work found a national audience through *DT*. And I also think of the number of young writers whose work first appeared in *DT*—Louise Erdrich and Carolyn Forché come immediately to mind. And those special chapbooks and anthologies: the 1974 collection of 50 poems by Tom McGrath entitled *Voices From Beyond the Wall*, published in a special arrangement with Swallow Press, one of the rare occasions when a large commercial press worked cooperatively with a small, non-commercial press; and the pioneering Native American anthology *The First Skin Around Me: Contemporary American Tribal Poetry*, edited by the late James L. White. Looking at the collective table of contents for the 17 issues of *DT* is like reading a registry of distinguished American poets—and through to their final issue, the editors remained true to their original mission statement: "We see ourselves, then, as importers and exporters, seeking the best work from both new and established writers no matter what their *place*— that unique vitality which partakes of both the local and international simultaneously."

Secondly—and not unrelated—is Vinz's involvement with Plains Distribution Service, Inc., a non-profit literary organization for the promotion and distribution of Midwestern authors and non-commercial presses. The brainchild of Joe Richardson and Vinz, Plains Distribution lasted from 1975-1981 and was a flagship literary organization in the United States. With annual budgets of over $100,000.00, Plains Distribution Service remains, even today, a unique, revolutionary idea for the promotion and distribution of contemporary literature. Again, a chronicle of that experiment can be found in Vinz's essay "Looking Back on Ten Years of *Dacotah Territory*" and in Joe Richardson's essay "Not a Little Magazine: Plains Distribution, *Dacotah Territory*, and the Publishing Game" (also in *Dacotah Territory: A Ten Year Anthology*). Looking back at its short and influential life, I still find its achievements impressive: the developing of 18 booklists advertising an average of 15 small press titles per list mailed to over 4,000 individuals, libraries, and bookstores; the sponsoring and organizing of a national small press distribution conference (May 1976, Fargo) attended by over 20 national and regional literary organizations; the sponsoring of The Plains Bookbus, that remarkable 35 foot modified recreational vehicle, which from 1977-1980 traveled to more than 200 stops at bookfairs, conferences, libraries, booksellers' conventions and colleges and universities throughout the Midwest to sell books, give workshops and seminars, and sponsored over 100 poetry and fiction readings. All of this done, in the words of Vinz, as "a constant and continuing advocacy of Midwestern authors and presses." The audience developed through the activities sponsored by Plains Distribution can never truly be measured, but it is safe to say its reach was far and wide.

In addition to his work as editor, publisher, literary entrepreneur and writer

(I've chosen not to comment here about Vinz's own poetry since the essay to follow examines his eight collections of poetry), Vinz is by profession and vocation an educator. It must be kept in mind that all the while Vinz was editing and publishing *Dacotah Territory* and involved with Plains Distribution, he was teaching writing and literature at Moorhead State University in Moorhead, Minnesota, where he is now Professor of English. And as if teaching at Moorhead State were not enough, Vinz carried his expertise and love of literature and poetry beyond the classroom to the community, specifically to the writers-in-the-schools programs in both North Dakota and Minnesota

Beginning in 1973 with his assistance in developing an NEA grant to help establish a Poets-in-the-Schools pilot project in Moorhead, Vinz has worked in Writers-in-the-Schools programs, K-12, from 1974-1988, totaling over 50 weeks of residencies in over 30 schools throughout rural and urban Minnesota and North Dakota. In many of these schools, Vinz was the first poet ever to visit and work with students in the area of creative writing. The thrust of these residencies was to provide positive language experiences for the students and to break down barriers and stereotypes. But perhaps even more important were the in-service workshops and seminars Vinz conducted for the teachers—the ones who shape curriculum. Vinz's skills as editor and publisher dovetailed neatly with his Writers-in-the-Schools work since one of the goals of residencies, for Vinz, was to see student work into print. Vinz's work has resulted in his editing of six anthologies of student poems, ranging from a collection of poems by 4th graders from Fargo's Creative Arts Studio to a statewide anthology of student poetry from the Minnesota Poets-in-the-Schools program. Needless to say, Vinz's journeyman work in the infancy of these state-wide programs has led to more doors opening for more writers and artists in the elementary and secondary schools of North Dakota and Minnesota.

I offer this catalog of achievements in the career of Mark Vinz (a career, by the way, which is far from over!) not so much to impress—though it does impress—but rather to introduce readers to Mark Vinz's contributions to contemporary literary culture of the upper Midwest. And I also want to suggest that there are hundreds of "Mark Vinzes" throughout the many regions of this country, who over the years, had a vision of what poetry and life could be, then, worked steadily and diligently in their quiet ways to realize that vision. If we recognize anything when we walk into a great cathedral it is that we are in the presence of someone—or some many—who possessed great vision: who imagined it then cared enough to follow it through to creation. Auden's comment to the contrary, poetry *does* make something happen, and Mark Vinz is among those who believe this. The book, I hope, will preserve and record the personal vision behind the edifice for our own times as well as for the future—lest we delegate the architect to anonymity. Elsen writes that "the function of the master builder was to conceive the plan...and to decide how to go about building the edifice." Such has been the work of Mark Vinz—and others like him—in the cathedral of poetry in the Midwest.

THE JOURNEY AND THE RETURN:
THE POETRY OF MARK VINZ

I

"Traveler, accept what you will—
I could never conjure this."

"From the Far Edge"

Mark Vinz was born in the geographical center of North America, Rugby, North Dakota, in 1942, and shortly thereafter moved with his family to Minneapolis, where he spent most of his childhood. In 1957 he moved to suburban Kansas City with his family. After taking B.A. and M.A. degrees in English from the University of Kansas, he moved to the Southwest where he studied at The University of New Mexico in Albuquerque from 1966 to 1968, working under the mentorship of Gene Frumkin. Except for his brief stint in the Southwest, Vinz has lived and worked all of his life in the heartland of America. Since 1968, Vinz has lived in Moorhead, Minnesota, with his wife, Betsy, and their two daughters, Katie and Sarah.

Mark Vinz has a vivid memory of hearing Langston Hughes giving a poetry reading at the University of Kansas in 1964. A 22-year-old former chemistry major turned English major at the time, Vinz recalls Hughes' reading with great warmth and appreciation. Since hearing his first poetry reading nearly twenty-five years ago, Vinz has authored six chapbooks of poems: *Winter Promises* (BkMk Press, 1975); *Letters to the Poetry Editor* (Capra Press, 1974); *Red River Blues* (Poetry-Texas, 1977); *Songs for a Hometown Boy* (Solo Press, 1977); *Contingency Plans (Ohio Review,* 1978); and *Deep Water, Dakota* (Juniper Press, 1980). And 1983 saw the publication of his first full-length collection, *Climbing the Stairs* (Spoon River Poetry Press) and *The Weird Kid* (New Rivers Press), which won a Minnesota Voices Project award. His poems have appeared in over one hundred magazines and anthologies, and his recent turn to fiction has been equally successful.

Winter Promises, Vinz's first collection, was published by Dan Jaffe at BkMk Press in Kansas City in 1975. Here we find two of Vinz's themes which—even today—continue to weave themselves throughout his work: the Midwest landscape and domestic life. Land and family—what other two themes so embody the Midwestern psyche? One touches the public self, the other the private; one the exterior, the other the interior.

Speakers in Vinz's Midwestern poems are scout-like in their experiencing the Midwestern landscape, always reporting back what they have discovered and have come to know as "truth." In their reports there is always a hint of as-

3

tonishment at the powers, mysteries, and unfathomable ambiguities that exist at the far edge:

> No one will believe the winters,
> the land as flat and broad
> as God's shinbone...   (*WP*, "For the Far Edge," p. 6)

Or from "Inland":

> What, after all, is a horizon?
>
> No one has mapped these shadows.
> No one will fence these winds.
>   (*WP*, p. 9)

Or from "Poem Written on the Back of an Official Memorandum":

> This is the territory we could never imagine.
>   (*WP*, p. 20)

Yet there is always more than astonishment in the message. There is also the life of the Plains, which is always meted out on its own terms. In a landscape that gives up little, Vinz is a patient looker and a gracious receiver of what it does offer. The fragments and glimpses of truth are like precious stones or charms to be cupped in the palm of the hand. For those willing to look hard beyond themselves, the landscape will offer its beauty:

> Just past Fargo, where the land
> falls way to a dream
> there are sharks diving in wheat—
> girls with thistles in their hair
> pearls and oak trees, herons, ladders, bells
>   (*WP*, "What We Know," p. 7)

Or from "Deserted Farm":

> Tomorrow the heavy lilac blossoms will open,
> higher than the roofbeams, reeling in wind.
>   (*WP*, p. 10)

And from "Prairie Song":

> clouds like heavy blossoms,
> the sudden lance of sunlight
> just there,

where the river bends
into a grove of tribal willow. (*WP*, p. 12)

Where:

Dragonflies maneuver through still sunlight
and the slow change is beginning.
Corona of dust
Slipping through the branches of trees.
(*WP*, "September Poem," p. 22)

These are not the great landscapes of this country—not the Appalachians, the Rockies, the Grand Canyon, the Pacific coasts of Oregon and Washington. But they are what is here; they are what the Plains offer. The journey-work of the stars can be found in prairie grass, too, and Vinz is capable of finding it.

Shadow and darkness are ever-present in Vinz's early poems as well as in the later work. Much has been written about the overuse of these words in contemporary poetry, yet they do seem so right as archetypes for the post-Hiroshima world. Vinz uses the words to suggest consciousness on the verge of descending to the underworld of self, that time in the human spirit when the soul is about to undergo transformation. Speakers in such situations abound in Vinz's poems, which often begin in twilight or late at night:

Grandfather,
I dream of you in the long Dakota night.
(*WP*, "Dream Song," p. 8)

Or in "Inland" which begins "Just before sunset" (p. 9) or in "Deserted Farm" where "decaying timbers moan softly in twilight" (p. 10). Travelers are often caught and eventually lost in the darkness: "we drive…into the roads that unroll suddenly before us,/into the long Dakota night" ("Primer Lesson," p. 15); or from "Night Letter, Night Song": "Just so, we travel through/our messages, alone:/calligraphy of moonlight/where our shadows touch our eyes" (p. 35). Though lacking the surreal and mystical shorthand of, say, Robert Bly, Vinz's poems in *Winter Promises* and *Red River Blues*, his third collection published in 1977, far from being imitative, are reminiscent of many of Bly's poems in *Silence in the Snowy Fields*.

Vinz's early poems have an "edgy" quality; there's a quietness, a contemplative and meditative aura about them which make us feel we are in the presence of something greater and deeper than ourselves. In these poems we are aware of the mythic depths of a landscape we are on the verge of stepping into and traveling through:

5

You are alone and moving,
one small beacon
inside white dark.
You have read your name
in every ditch,
on every tree and sign.   (*RRB*, "Traveling Home," p. 14)

Or in "Ritual," where "the darkness grows heavy/with the ceremony of
their secret singing" (*RRB*, p. 8). And from "Driving Through":

Tell yourself it doesn't matter now,
you're only driving through...
toward the great dark of the fields...
—still undelivered,
enroute for years.   (*RRB*, p. 5)

Like *Winter Promises*, *Red River Blues* is a study in landscape—this time
the winter landscape of the Red River Valley of the North where "you remember wind chill—40, 50, 60 below" and "after a point it ceases to matter"
("Still Life with Thermometer," p. 15). *Red River Blues'* voice is that of one
on the verge of stepping off the edge, of drifting into sleep, of letting go, of
moving toward a "place where all directions cease" ("Red River Blues," p. 4).
The thirteen poems in this chapbook are chilly, shadowy, and dark, like the
long prairie night that fascinates Vinz. Yet for all of its bleakness, *Red River
Blues* ends not on a note of despair but rather on a lyrical upturn, where a father and his children dance "the frozen rivers home,/bright summer feathers in
[their] hair" ("A Song for the Coldest Day," p. 16).

For all of his chilled, bleak landscapes, for all of his characters about to
step into shadowy territories of the self, Vinz never leaves us without hope.
Six years after the publication of *Red River Blues*, these very same themes remain at the core of his first full-length collection, *Climbing the Stairs*. Com-
fort and strength are still possible in Vinz's shadowy world:

It is so unfamiliar
to walk simply, one foot before the other,
for this is the world it is impossible to fall out of
•   •   •   •   •   •   •
a land turtle waking inside
inside his shell,
certain of nothing but
the strange new tide
surging over him,

6

ready at last to begin
(*CTS*, "Into the Dark," p. 70)

And the traveler, unsure of his journey in "In a Drought Year," knows that he is "going nowhere/but going home" (p. 71). The possibilities for transformation, for self-discovery, have no geographical boundaries; climate and landscape are metaphors, finally, for the climates and regions of the soul.

II

"Tell us,
What shrinks?
Everything."

"Alma Mater"

The title poem of *Songs for a Hometown Boy* (1977) is dedicated to "all the hometown boys/I've ever known.../or been" (p. 7). This sequence of thirteen poems—along with eight others which make up this collection—seems as much therapeutical as anything else. The book is both homage to and exorcism of all those lost souls who inhabit small Midwestern towns; all of the hometown ghosts that follow us throughout our lives; all those awkward childhood moments; all our childhood friends who grow into men and women who never leave town, only to become the local drunks and "characters." All the time trying to convince us of the "rightness" of their lives:

Everybody has a tale to share—
the finest people on the earth,
you say, and say again into your beer.
You always leave before the lights come on.
("Songs for a Hometown Boy," p. 11)

The people and landscapes in this collection are out of Edward Hopper: the diner; the motel; the corner bars; worn men in caps, sad and tired like the waitresses who serve them coffee. The locale is Winesburg and Spoon River; the people are the people we might have been—save for some stroke of luck—or the people we are. This small but important collection is Vinz's

7

"Songs of Innocence and Experience." Putting these memories to rest is painful, for we invariably bury part of ourselves: "Now I cling to silence—/weatherless—/and the childhood dark" (A Burial," p. 21).

. . . . . .

Mythical Midwestern towns populated by plain-speaking folk and eccentrics: every Midwestern writer is inevitably drawn to this idiom. Anderson, Cather, Masters. And of Vinz's contemporaries, I think of Dave Etter's *Alliance, Illinois*; Ted Kooser's *Cottonwood County*; William Kloefkorn's *Alvin Turner* and *ludi jr*. Three years after *Songs for a Hometown Boy*, Vinz returned to his fascination with the small Midwestern town in his mythical *Deep Water, Dakota*—but this time as a tourist, not a permanent resident. "The Town Crier" is our tour guide to Deep Water, introducing us to the whole crew, the/displaced people of Deep Water, Dakota": the railroad man, the gambler, the homesteaders, the first lady, the fallen preacher's son, the spinster women, Old Doc, and the Nighthawk—"the crazy lady loaded up with/lint and shopping bags," who is eventually replaced by the retired night desk editor of the *Fargo Forum*. *Deep Water, Dakota* is a collection that could have been more, that could have pushed Vinz to the limits of his version of this Midwestern idiom. But in such an idiom, there is always the possibility of redundancy—yet it's a risk one must take. Perhaps Vinz will return to Deep Water, Dakota, someday, for I suspect he never really left.

In a quirky and delightful collection called *Letters to the Poetry Editor*, (1975), Vinz abandoned the Midwestern landscape for a brief trip into parody. Vinz described the genesis of this humorous collection:

> done with some pain, all based loosely on the kinds of letters
> little magazine editors so often discover with submissions (or
> from reading between the verses); and which I began as a kind of
> necessary valve to let off some editorial frustration.

Written during the early years when Vinz edited *Dacotah Territory* (reading hundreds of manuscripts, I suspect, every month), this collection is not so much parody of individuals as it is parody of trendiness in contemporary poetry. *Letters to the Poetry Editor* exposes us to our sometimes wrongheadedness about the way we conduct ourselves as poets. As Vinz writes of the many types: "…we all have probably been [one] at one time or another." Here we find letters from the confessional poet (from Decatur, Illinois), who

8

doesn't have much to confess; the suffering poet, who writes and *asks* for a rejection slip; the self-inflated poet, who is sure the editor recognizes his or her name; the nature poet, who "thrives/on wild food and all the/organic things"; the "fellow regionalist," who includes a mystical sequence to windmill and water tank; and the ethnic poet, who instructs the editor to check the enclosed list for whatever type of ethnic poem he would like to see. At first, *Letters to the Poetry Editor* seems an anomaly in Vinz's work during the last twelve years, but Vinz's wit and his ability to parody show up with consistency and frequency throughout his work, especially in his most recent collection, *The Weird Kid* (1983), a collection of whimsical and playful dreamscapes and meditations on childhood.

The intensity with which Vinz stalks a theme or subject—which is so pervasive in his early collections—eases, to some degree, in his latest collections, *Climbing the Stairs* and *The Weird Kid*, (both 1983). Vinz possesses a fine sense of the comic; his ability to parody is first-rate, whether he is discoursing on discount department stores where "shoppers live [beneath the store] and study muzak" ("Discount Shopping," p. 39, *CTS*) or mumbling about a starlet on a late night talk show who chatters vacuously about how she "gets into vegetables" because "they're so easy to relate to'" ("Talk Show," p. 38, *CTS*). Ultimately, Vinz exposes our frailty, despite our attempts to camouflage it with intelligence and sophistication. The prose poems in *The Weird Kid* demonstrate this best of all. The title poem of the collection explores the archetype of the weird kid, "the martyr we could always count on to take the heat off everyone else"; the one who "ooz[ed] ink, cowlicks, and ripped seams, and tardy slips" (p. 68); the class clown, the fool, the one within whom Vinz allows us to see a part of ourselves. Of Vinz's work in *Climbing the Stairs*, poet Tom McGrath writes that "the unwary reader is likely to get hooked on an off-beat view of the quotidian and of *place*—something Vinz does better than anyone I know. A better reader will see the persona as a solitary man doing a tight-rope walk (balanced on one side by loneliness and on the other side by his losses) just above the Void— and doing it with wit and grace." McGrath's characterization of Vinz's tragicomic Chaplinesque view of the world underscores a constant found throughout Vinz's eight collections of poems published during the past fifteen years.

III

> *"In this which is called a house...*
> *My friends, my love,*
> *so little changes.*
> *If I rage in the morning*
> *there are still the windless fields*
>   *of afternoon*
>   (*CTS*, "Letter to the Outside," p. 21)

> *"If for a moment,*
> *be welcome here."*
>   (*CTS*, "Sleepwalking," p. 3)

Domestic life: family, love, responsibility to self and others, holding the center together, living in your own country, controlling internal affairs, adapting to human living conditions. In all of his work, Vinz is a writer struggling to know what it means to be a father, a husband, a lover, a friend. And he is intent on rooting out the answer—if there is one. Yet Vinz seems not to be troubled when the search turns up empty. Observing his children, Vinz writes: "Their eyes look out/from deep within their shells/where we cannot see them" (*WP*, "The Children," p. 30). And after a walk along the Red River concludes: "Later, we will come back.../and watch the islands floating past us/toward places we cannot go" (*WP*, "Walking By the Red River," p. 31). Perhaps that knowledge alone is enough explanation.

Vinz is always trying to return "home," that mythical place which invariably changes the moment we leave. By doing so, he hopes to recover some bit of memory, some clue that just might explain it all, tell him who he was and is:

> This was your bed,
> your lamp, your chair,
> the western windows
> hung with promises
> against the gathering dusk.
> You wait for something
> beautiful to write about
> • • • • • • • • • • • • • •
> What was it that held you here,
> and drives you back—
>   (*RRB*, "Going Back," p. 11)

10

And in "A Dream of Fish," Vinz tries to grasp the quick flashes of childhood memory which elude him like silvery fish: "Childhood is that place you visit often now...Deep down other shapes are moving—" (*CTS*, p. 12). But it is not as though he comes away empty handed:

> What is it you have learned?
> That you have traveled far enough
> to start the journey back.
> That your promises rise and fall
> with weather, seasons, tides.
> <div align="right">(<i>CP</i>, "Libra," p. 86)</div>

The meaning he culls from experience is this: that life is a struggle, both private and shared; that there is fear of loss and of failure, and the fear of "going down"; that there is grief and loneliness; that there is pain and sorrow; that we are, for the most part, alone in the journey. Yet "something holds us here," in midcontinent, in our geographical lives as well as in our psychological lives. And that "something" is love, always, holding us here. And finally, that the only guarantee is the undiscovered self, waiting to be found.

IV

"Something seems to be stirring out there in the dark fields."
(TWK, "Still Life: The Pleasures of
Home," p. 53)

And what of the work to come? In two unpublished manuscripts, Vinz struggles with grief, suffering, and loss, appropriate themes for one entering mid-life, where family, friends, and colleagues grow old with us. I think we will see Vinz struggling with what is means to be male in our society, as well as exploring male-female relationships. We'll see Vinz approaching these themes with the same tough, rigorous, and unrelenting passion that we have seen him approach Midwest landscape and domestic life themes in his previous work. And I think we'll see Vinz always asking the same question: "what is it worth/to have known the/dark beneath each step/ and footfall?' (*CTS*, "Climbing the Stairs," p. 17). The answers, I think, will be the same: it is worth everything.

Despite his constant reworking of Midwestern themes in all of his collections, Vinz continues to yield a bountiful harvest of insightful poems. In his future work, I believe Mark Vinz will continue to examine, explore, and analyze what it means to live in this country as a Midwesterner. His working of the Midwestern landscape will continue, I think, to be central in his poetry. And I do not think he need fear repetition or redundancy. For as I have tried to suggest, Vinz possesses the uncanny ability to uncover and reveal something new, a unique perspective, every time he takes up the Midwestern landscape as a subject. His working of this theme, his writing and turning of this theme, reminds me of the way the medieval philosopher turned the philosopher's stone in his hand, over and over, trying to penetrate its secret, knowing all the while that part of its mystery is that the stone can never be fully penetrated. But that very act of focusing, of centering, is where insight and transcendence reside. And knowing this is what wisdom truly means.

Books by Mark Vinz

Winter Promises. Shawnee Mission, Kansas: BkMk. Press, 1975. Also includes the chapbook *Wild Onions* by Daniel Lusk. (Out of print)

Letters to the Poetry Editor. Santa Barbara, CA.: Capra Press, 1975; reprinted in *The Capra Chapbook Anthology*, 1979.

Red River Blues. Texas City, Texas: Poetry Texas, 1977. (Out of print)

Songs for a Hometown Boy. San Louis Obispo, CA.: Solo Press, 1977.

Contingency Plans. Athens, Ohio: *The Ohio Review*, Vol. xix, No. 3. Fall, 1978. A special chapbook insert.

Deep Water, Dakota. La Crosse, WI.: Juniper Press, 1980.

Climbing the Stairs. Peoria, IL.: Spoon River Poetry Press, 1983.

The Weird Kid. St. Paul, MN.: New Rivers Press, 1983.

Great River Review. Volume Seven, No. 1, 1986 "Featured Poet."

Mixed Blessings. Peoria, IL.: Spoon River Poetry Press, 1989.

Books and Magazines Edited by Mark Vinz

Dacotah Territory Magazine, Nos. 1-17, 1971-81; also editor or associate editor for Territorial Press, including the *Dacotah Territory* Chapbook Series (12 short collections of poems by individuals) and 3 full-length collections of poetry.

Dacotah Territory: A Ten Year Anthology. Fargo, ND: North Dakota Institute for Regional Studies, 1982. Edited with Grayce Ray.

An Explosion of White Petals: An Anthology of Student Poetry from the Minnesota Poets in the Schools Program, 1978-79. St. Paul, MN: COMPAS, 1979.

Scribbling on a Star: Writing from the North Dakota Writers-in-Schools Program, 1977-80. Fargo, ND: North Dakota Council on the Arts, 1981.

Sparks in the Dark: Student Writing from the North Dakota Writers-in-Residence Program, Part II, 1981-82 (Part I, 1980-81, edited by Joan Eades). Fargo, ND: North Dakota Council on the Arts, 1983.

Stirring the Deep:
A Conversation with Mark Vinz

The first version of this interview was recorded at Blue Sky Resort near Detroit Lakes, Minnesota, in late August of 1984. It has since been expanded and reshaped in three other sessions.

Tammaro: In a 1974 interview that you conducted with Tom McGrath, John Milton and Frederick Manfred, which eventually was published in an issue of *Dacotah Territory*, you talked about regional writing and suggested two directions that you saw regional writing take. The first direction was a concern for local color, a kind of provincialism, isolationism, and boosterism. And then the second direction, which I think is one that probably you felt the good regional writing comes out of, is that the region is a place where one discovers sources, the land, its history, its past, and then a particular place. And then you go on to quote Donald Davidson—a line from one of his books that was published in 1938: "As a people in this country"—and I'll quote him—"our healthy identity as individuals is related to place." So how do you feel about those statements more than ten years down the line? You've been writing poems during that time and have been heavily involved in poetry of place and regionalism.

Vinz: I still feel basically committed to them, though I've learned some things, too. I think I've lost some of my zeal, partly because when I was editing *Dacotah Territory* and becoming very interested in *place*, I was making certain discoveries, and when you do that you tend perhaps to take a more extreme view. I still think that in many ways the health in contemporary writing is in its diversity, and that in turn quite often is tied to specific regions of the country. Place is where many writers learn to write, to discover the concrete, which is a being aware of the life that's going on around them and not having to fake it and not having to blast off somewhere that they're not familiar with. I see this a great deal in student writing. Students think there's nothing to write about in the little town they're from, so they end up writing fantasy or science fiction or something that's terribly unconvincing. So I think that at any level, whether you're talking about beginning writers or

15

whether you're talking about fully accomplished writers, that sense of being tied into and aware of particular places and regions is still a source of a great deal of strength and health and diversity. This is a country of regions and I really distrust greatly the notion that we have a national culture. If we *do* have a national culture, it's a culture of the mass media.

Tammaro: What about that first part of that definition? It seems to be more of a pejorative definition, that is local color, provincialism, isolationism. These are words that you used. Can you talk about that a little bit?

Vinz: I still think that's a great danger. Regionalism, or writing with the emphasis on place, is very much a double-edged sword. If it can lead to healthy diversity and discovery on the one hand, then there's always the danger of complacency and being cut off and becoming simply a booster or becoming simply a landscape artist, so to speak. Something else that I've discovered in the last few years is that sometimes you can have a "militant" regionalism, where all things become judged exclusively by adherence to region or fidelity to a particular ethnic group, and so on. The way Davidson talked about it is that regionalism is healthy when it happens unself-consciously, when the artist draws upon it naturally. It becomes unhealthy the more self-conscious it gets.

Tammaro: That was leading me to the next question. In an interview or an essay, you mentioned something about one of the negative concerns that you have with regional writing. And I suspect this results from editing a magazine like *Dacotah Territory* that had at its beginnings the intention to be an exporter of regional writers and to publish some new writers in the region. You mentioned the idea of self-conscious regionalism, and perhaps that's what you're aiming at there, that sense of isolating yourself and writing out of a false sense of regionalism.

Vinz: Sometimes at the *expense of*—you know, you're saying that "my place is better than...."

Tammaro: And in the book *Letters to the Poetry Editor* you touched on that in one of those little satirical poems about the poet who writes from New York to say:

16

Dear Editor:

I am an ethnic poet. Here are 42 Chicano poems, all written during my visit to El Paso last month. Should you not find these interesting, I will be happy to send you more work. Please indicate your preferences, according to the following list:

American Indian (specify tribe)
Black (specify degree of militancy)
Eskimo
Jewish
New England Fisherman
North Dakota Farmer (specify crop)
Polish Ghetto
Southwestern Adobe
Other....................

P.S.   My first book of poems will be available soon. It's called *Twenty Aztec Verses and A Leaping Scandinavian Quartet.*

That's probably from your sense of reading so many what you may call false regional poems, or self-conscious regional poems.

Vinz: Yes, that's part of it, but there's a second part, too—if something seems to be "hot," or if a particular magazine is publishing a certain kind of poem, there seem to be several people willing to write to those specifications. You might call it putting on the necessary mask. For example, in our Native American issue of *Dacotah Territory*, we inadvertently published some poems by a man who was not an Indian. We found out about it much later, that he had successfully tricked the editors by putting on an Indian mask just to get published. There's another kind of false regionalism that comes to mind, too— what Tom McGrath calls "nature fakery." The wonderful lakes and woods of Minnesota are fine, and provide great inspiration for poets of all kinds, but if all one does is simply go out in the woods and quiver and write about trees, one is giving up something. So, drawing on place can be a dangerous thing. It has to be something one does with a kind of balance.

Tammaro: You have another poem in *Letters to the Poetry Editor* about the regional poet. Maybe you could read that one.

Vinz: This is again tied into that same theme.

XX. Dear Fellow Regionalist:

I too am known as
Follower of Earth and Sky!
I thought you'd like to see
the fruits enclosed:

a sequence (mystical)
to windmill and water tank,
3 bear songs and a cattail fugue,
a passage from a history in verse
of pioneers in Filmore County
and surrounding acreage,
and last, my 16 portraits
of a neighbor's Uncle Josh
at work with Red Man snuff
and whittling knife.

The thing I was trying to get in that poem is that strong writing of place is more than a given set of images. Because you write a poem about the Midwest that happens to have a Holstein in it, does it mean that that's a good poem? There's a certain iconography that's very easy to learn. But good writing is always more than that. It's always more than knowing simply which images to evoke.

Tammaro: While we're on the subject of region and place, what are some of your own ideas about poetry and place, for example, in your own work? You were born in North Dakota, and you've lived in Minneapolis, and you've lived in Kansas, and you've lived in New Mexico. I guess my question would be how have those places affected your own writing over the past fifteen years?

Vinz: I think when I really started writing seriously it was making a certain set of discoveries about myself and trying to write a kind of poem that was more than private—that had other kinds

18

of images in it. And I think that is the first thing that a writer has to learn. I happened to discover that from places, from childhood, from memory, and even from living in a place that at the time seemed very alien and inhospitable to me, but that I eventually came, I suppose, to understand. I lived in New Mexico for a very short time—for two years. And I never really did do much writing about New Mexico and the writing I did always displeased me because it was what I called tourist poetry. I had the sense that every poem I wrote someone else had written, or perhaps many people had written the same poem. It wasn't *my* place, whereas the Upper Midwest *is* my place. And I think the more I began to discover, think and remember, the more richness I found, the more things to write about, and I began to feel comfortable with it. I think it goes back again to that idea of being self-conscious. When I was in New Mexico I was terribly self-conscious about writing. Here, over the years, I think I've evolved something very different.

Tammaro: What are your thoughts about the role of poetry and place in contemporary poetry?

Vinz: I think it's still very important. In my own work it seems whether I'm writing anything that has to do with place or not, place is always kind of an anchor. It's always something I go back to. I just finished teaching an Elderhostel course that dealt with the prairie. Naturally, I've written a couple of prairie poems. But I hadn't written any place poems for along time. I guess I see that true of a lot of writers. Several years ago John Milton did a special issue of *South Dakota Review* which was a symposium in which he had written to about 80 different writers and asked them to respond to the impact of place on their own work. And the overwhelming majority said that their own work was grounded in one way or another in place, and maybe in very similar ways to my own experience. A few said, "No, my commitment is to internationalism or something else." I see that true in American poetry in general. I think there are still number of fine writers who are tied in some of their best work to those places. I see it happening more often in the Midwest, or in the Southwest, or the Pacific Northwest, and in the deep South—again, regions that traditionally have had that kind of tie. I see it happening far less on the West coast or on the East coast, where place doesn't seem to be nearly as important as certain other things. I feel right now that American poetry is very diverse. I also think sometimes that the best poems are the ones that don't get the recognition that they should, and that Midwestern writers who are tied into place sometimes are at a disadvantage because they're not very trendy, they're not very stylish.

Tammaro: I'm thinking of the August, 1984 issue of *Harper's Magazine*; there was a special forum called "Naming the Land" in honor of the Academy of American Poets which was celebrating its fiftieth birthday. The editor states that *Harper's* publishes 15 poems reflecting "the passion to explore the American text." And there's the little quote from Whitman about the United States being the greatest poem. The introduction to the article says, " But whether the poets locate their greatest poem in the landscape or a city street, a filling station, or a neighborhood front yard, all of them practice what William Carlos Williams called the 'poet's business not to talk in vague categories, but to write in particular.'" And then you begin to read the poems and the poets in there are very fine poets. But what's noticeably missing form that group of 15 poets are the poets who I have come to see or I have discovered, poets who I think have been working for many, many years—10, 20, 30 years, who have been working in the landscape of the Midwest, the Upper Midwest, the West. Poets in whose work landscape is very much part of their poems. Yet those people are not in that representation. And my feeling is: where are the James Hearsts, where are the Bill Staffords, where are the Ted Koosers? You don't see them there and this is *Harper's Magazine*. And so someone who reads this magazine and may see this poem by James Merrill or Derek Walcott, and think that these are the people who are doing the pioneering work in poetry of place and regionalism, and I think that's very misleading. It seems to me, anyway, to be very misleading. And I kept turning page after page waiting for a Ted Kooser or a Bill Stafford poem or a number of other poets whose names we could rattle off— Dave Etter comes to mind—who have been committed to the Midwestern landscape as the vital resource for their poetry— For example, where's Wendell Berry who has committed himself and who is very insightful? Yet they're omitted from here and I'm a little bit disturbed by that.

Vinz: Well, I think it goes back again to that idea of what's fashionable, of what's trendy. There's still that feeling in most of us that regional means local, local means cut off or second class or "not as good." Again, I think some of the poets who are getting the most national acclaim right now are the poets whose work has very little, if anything, to do with place. I guess I go back to people like Donald Davidson in sharing that distrust of that kind of national culture. You know, something else that bothers me goes far beyond poetry, and that is also something that Davidson wrote about in the 30's. I really do see him as a kind of prophet. He talked about an increasing sense of homelessness in American culture, of placelessness as our society becomes more interchangeable, and as living becomes more suburban—there's a kind of sameness, there's a loss of certain connections, of roots, of memories. I read an interview with William Goyen years ago in *Paris Review* and he was talking about teaching at Princeton and asking his students to write about a place, and they didn't know what he was talking about. And he kept saying, "Don't you have anything, isn't there something—a tree—anything you remember?" Instead of writing about generalized pain, or generalized love, or something similar. If you look at our great writers, you know, there are many people who are very tied to place—Faulkner, Cather, Twain, Flannery O'Connor, any number of them. They're writers of place. I guess one other thing I'd add as a footnote: regionalism, poetry of place, whatever you want to call it, can reflect many different kinds of places. One's place, one's identity, one's past, one's ethnicity—it's all part of the same thing. It's a mistake to think that place means simply rural. One's sense of place comes out of where one is, where one has grown up, what's shaped the individual. And that, in far more cases than not, is *not* rural.

Tammaro: The terms that you use—"sense of place" and "concept of home"—were trendy topics years ago—perhaps maybe we've exhausted that and so we need to move on to something else, I don't know—but I think sometimes academia has a tendency to grab onto an idea and then run with it until it's exhausted and then try to hook onto some new trendy or chic idea. And I think writers eventually get caught up in that trend, too.

Vinz: That's very true. Throughout our culture we tend to get very

21

preoccupied by certain things—to the point of exhaustion. On the other hand, one simply shouldn't discard certain things either. For example, a few years ago Native American literature became very "hot"—a number of anthologies were published, and perhaps we became a bit too absorbed by things Indian. However, that absorption brought many talented writers into print, revived many important ideas. And from it, many things of value remain. In that sense, perhaps all the hoopla over *place* has indeed been exhausting in some circles, yet it has also been a necessary preoccupation, bringing certain ideas, writers, and publications into view. It's been a very useful dialogue and needs to be a recurring one—beyond fashion and beyond chic. In my own work, too, I've found myself becoming far too self-conscious about things such as *place*. Yet while place is something I'm not particularly preoccupied with any more, those questions and those connections still remain very important to me and to my development as a writer. In that vein, too, I must say that the relationship between literature and place needs to be much more than the evocation of a landscape. It is a connection to something larger—that's the essential point here. Here's a *place* poem called "North of North" that I wrote a couple of years ago, after consciously avoiding writing that kind of poem for three or four years. In that regard it marked an important *return* for me. In one sense it's about living in a certain region or landscape, but it's also—I hope—about something that transcends that landscape.

> Today with no surprise
> the wind chill sinks to 50 below.
> The mailman slouches up the walk,
> head down, the way we all learn how
> to walk on this far edge.
> You write to say how cold it must be here,
> and thank whatever gods you have
> this weather's north of you, far north.
>
> But we say it too—
> it's always colder somewhere else.
> We praise our plows and furnaces,
> fall back again on what we know:
> there are no last words,

and what we speak of
is neither storm nor chill,
but what would happen if all letters stopped—
that other winter, directionless,
colder than ice, deeper than snow.

Ah, those wonderful Moorhead days with 50 below wind chill, when you have to ask yourself what you're doing living in a place like this, and then getting a letter from a friend who lives in the South and has seen the weather reports for the Upper Midwest. You try to respond. There's cold weather here, sure, but there's another kind of cold, too. You know, the freezing up of human relations and communication.

Tammaro: The landscape then becomes a way into the inner life and becomes much more a vehicle rather than the thing itself.

Vinz: It ultimately becomes a kind of metaphor.

Tammaro: And so finally you end up leaving that literal landscape and getting into that metaphorical landscape. What you're seeing in a lot of those manuscripts as the editor of *Dacotah Territory*, perhaps, is a lot of poems that stop at that literal level. Here's a barn and a silo and a frozen cow out in the plain, and that's it. But never a sense of what's happening inside the writer.

Vinz: It becomes all very quaint and picturesque and so on, but not much more than that. You know, I mentioned John Milton, the editor of *South Dakota Review*, who has done some tremendously important work in the past 25 years of editing that magazine. He has a marvelous essay called "The Dakota Image," where he talks about the same thing we've been talking about—this idea of place and how different writers over the years have seen the Dakotas and the Upper Midwest in general. And it's his thesis, and mine too, that a great deal of the best Midwest writing turns on a kind of love/hate relationship. You know, there are good, positive things about living here and there are some very harsh, negative things. The best poems tend to be those that take into account that diversity—the beauty and the harshness together. Without this balance you can fall off either into cynicism on one hand or simply apolo-

23

getics and boosterism on the other. The poets I prize the most, whose writing comes out of the Midwest and touches on Midwest places, are those who have attained that balance in one way or another. To me that's a very important quality of Midwest writing in general. Though, of course, it's not limited to the Midwest.

Tammaro: When you teach Midwestern literature, whose poems do you use to illustrate that idea? You see that love/hate tension in many writers—novelists—you see it a great deal in Midwestern novels, of wanting to be a part of the New York scene or wanting to be someplace else, not being appreciated in their own hometown, or state. Yet at the same time they love the place where they are.

Vinz: Well, you can start any number of places. I might start with William Stafford, who's a native Midwesterner growing up in Hutchinson, Kansas, and who's written many poems about that idea of going back and coming away. There's a tremendous tension there between roots and expatriation.

Tammaro: "The Farm on the Great Plains," perhaps.

Vinz: Yes, that would be a very good example. I think too of Tom McGrath's "The Buffalo Coat," when he thinks back to his grandfather and the pioneers, and their "wildness" as opposed to the tameness he sees now, where everything's paved over. So there's another kind of tension. In this case it's past versus present.

Tammaro: That's the sense, then, of discovering the region as a source, of looking at the land or its history. It can be personal history.

Vinz: I think there are many of those kinds of tensions. The harshness and beauty of the landscape is one, but there are many others when one starts thinking of one's personal history and the history of place and the pioneer past. Again, I'll use McGrath because I think he's a real oracle on this subject. He talks about living simultaneously within a strong sense of three cultures. First, the culture past—the pioneers in the Midwest—the whole agrarian past, the homesteading. Second, the Indians and their way of life. And third, the present culture. Quite often in his poems, Richard Lyons, who also lived for many years in Fargo, wrote eloquently on this subject: the divisions between the different cultures—past and present, what's gained, what's lost. So I think you could go to any number of poets and find those kinds of dualities turned into some very exciting poems.

Tammaro: Who are the important contemporary Midwestern poets that you're most interested in now? Having edited *Dacotah Territory* for ten years you may be one of the more qualified people to make such a statement. Maybe you could begin with some important Midwestern poets and move out from there.

Vinz: Well, I certainly have nothing but the highest regard for Tom McGrath. He's been my teacher and my friend. He taught me a great deal about poetry. He's a poet who isn't nearly as well known in this country as he should be. Perhaps that's because of his politics. When I think of Midwestern poets I guess I *have* to think of McGrath. I also have to think of Bill Stafford, who's a man who has not lived in the Midwest for several years and yet who writes, perhaps, more eloquently about the Midwest than just about anybody I can think of. Another poet I admire greatly is Ted Kooser in Lincoln. I think he's one of the best younger poets today. I see tremendous diversity in his work: his personal history, the history of place, his humor, his skills as a craftsman. Moving on from there, I've had the kind of luxury of reading many poets and admiring them and then getting to know them.

Tammaro: One of the pluses of being an editor.

Vinz: A tremendous plus. Going to visit them or having them visit you. John Judson and Bob Schuler in Wisconsin, again poets whose influences have been very heavily oriental and who are writing a kind of meditative, quiet, beautiful, precise poetry that's very different from, let's say, a McGrath poem. Talking again about the diversity, these are poets that I have a great deal of respect for. Dan Jaffe in Kansas City, who came from the East Coast, a very different culture, and went to Nebraska and then to Kansas City, has any number of poems which I love. Dan was my first editor and also taught me a great deal.

Tammaro: Jaffe has been one of the major influences in the Midwest. He published many young Midwestern poets through BkMk

26

Press, which published *Winter Promises* in '75. It was your first book. So that's interesting that you mentioned that because he is a writer as well as a publisher. And I was just thinking—you mentioned John Judson who has Juniper Press and Bob Schuler who had Uzzano Press. And it seems that having a press and being a publisher are sort of a natural extension of the practice of the art of poetry and that's very common in the Midwest. And no one seems to think anything—that there's any difference between—it's just a natural outgrowth. I hadn't realized that until you began mentioning it. Tom McGrath had *Crazy Horse* magazine. Ted Kooser had Windflower Press. So maybe the sense of involvement in poetry and making fine books are things that happen here in the Midwest.

Vinz: I think so.

Tammaro: As you mentioned before, it's a kind of Midwestern independence, a do-it-myselfism kind of feeling.

Vinz: I think that the reason why I'm attracted to these people is first, I admire them as writers a great deal, and certainly as editors. But also, I admire the fact that they're nurturers, with a tremendous generosity of spirit. They are always willing to help, willing to labor to bring out new books, to discover new voices.

Tammaro: Like the old Midwestern barn raising. Maybe this is an equivalent: poetry raising!

Vinz: I think that's a good analogy.

Tammaro: Cooperation in the spirit of cooperation. If your neighbor is sick, you'll go over and harvest his crop and think nothing of it because eventually some day you're going to be sick and you're going to need your crop harvested. I think that's an important quality that I have certainly found to be true about the Midwest. There is a sense of community, and not necessarily community that's measured by distance, but perhaps a community that's measured by commitment.

Vinz: Well, maybe if we lived closer to each other we wouldn't like each other! Anyway, there *are* so many. I would definitely add two Illinois poets whose work I've admired, who've been an influence on me. One is Dave Etter. I think he, along with Bill Kloefkorn of Nebraska, has the best *ear* in Midwestern poetry. What he can do in capturing dialogue and rendering the idiom is absolutely splendid. The other would be John Knoepfle, who has written so diversely about so many things, going back to years and years ago when he interviewed the...

Tammaro: ...old boat men down in Cincinnati.

Vinz: Right. As well as a number of other directions.

Tammaro: Yes, his "Catholic poems" explore the Roman Catholic tradition.

Vinz: Knoepfle is himself a good example of the diversity possible in the Midwest. I'd add Ralph Mills of Chicago. He is an absolutely firstrate critic, who has also written some excellent criticism of contemporary poetry. We need more critics of his caliber.

Tammaro: Well, what are some of your feelings about what's been going on in contemporary poetry, let's say in the years since you've edited *Dacotah Territory*.

Vinz: Can we back up before we get into that?

Tammaro: Sure.

Vinz: There are a couple more poets that I've been wanting to mention. I think it would be hard to talk about the Midwest and not mention Robert Bly—a Midwestern poet who's attained international prominence. I was fortunate enough to meet and get to know Robert Bly when I first came back to Minnesota. He was also an editor and translator, and he helped me out a great deal in the early years with *Dacotah Territory*. Along with Bly, James Wright, a Midwestern poet whose Ohio poems are very different from his Minnesota-based poems. He was a marvelous poet, as was Jim White, a very, very, dear friend, a man whose work in the last years of his life dealt very frankly with his homosexuality, and who wrote a kind of poem that we couldn't call Midwestern in the same ways that we could the poems of other writers. Yet his poems *were* Midwestern. They were set in the honky-tonks of Indianapolis and among the street walkers in South Minneapolis.

Tammaro: One of the best Indiana poems that I've read is a poem of his called "Anderson, Indiana" that begins with two young Hoosiers shooting basketball out in the driveway at dusk, which if you've ever lived or passed through Indiana, you'll find all over the place. And it's just the perfect image. The poem settles into and ends in a very, very bleak image of Jim's experience growing up. It's a beautiful poem. It's also in the Stryk anthology of heartland poets.

Vinz: Stryk showed us in the *Heartland* anthologies some of the talent and diversity in Midwestern writing. We could go on mentioning names for a long time but also should point out that in spite of the distances between us there is still a real sense of communication and community among us. You can certainly see this in Midwestern writers' conferences and festivals, such as the one Phil Dacey put together in Marshall, Minnesota, in May of 1986.

Tammaro: That's the community. That's what I think is important. Bill Stafford has a wonderful line about what it is to be a writer. He says it's a gathering of writers and editors and publishers who get together, not out of deals and stealth, but because of their commitments and their own love for the art. And he sees *that* as their community.

Vinz: I would have to add one more name, and that's Richard Hugo, who was not a Midwesterner *per se*, but who was one of the most generous people I think I've ever known, a true teacher in the very best sense of the word.

Tammaro: I use Hugo a lot when I teach how a writer can take the particular place and use it to get at the universal, the mythical, to get inside the heart. All those beautiful, very human poems of sad Montana towns. Ultimately they are very human poems. But they're grounded in that locale, yet they're not about that locale. They're about the landscape of the human heart. He's a master of that.

Vinz: Years ago Tom McGrath made a statement somewhere that was quoted in the wrong context: "Dakota is everywhere." And I think when it got re-quoted the person who was quoting it

29

thought that this was a very egotistical, narrow-minded thing to say. What Tom meant is, I think, exactly what you're talking about: that he may be writing a poem that goes back to his boyhood on a farm in Sheldon, North Dakota. But what he's also writing about is not limited to North Dakota; it's about the problems of the human heart. It may be the struggles of the working class or it may be the fact that they're paving over all the good land. Those are problems that happen in North Dakota, but they also happen everywhere. And Tom believes that a good poem is simultaneously local and international. Cleanth Brooks also said he thought a good poem was universal on one end and particular on the other.

Tammaro: That certainly describes the best of Hugo's poems, whether he's writing about Scotland, Montana, or Washington.

Vinz: And to see Hugo labeled, as I have seen recently, as simply a Montana poet...

Tammaro: ...is really unfair, limiting, and a misreading of Hugo.

Vinz: He's a poet who used Montana as the basis for much of his work, but there again, he's certainly not *limited* to Montana anymore than McGrath is by North Dakota or Kooser is by Nebraska. There are two poets I also want to mention who are not Midwestern, who I admire very much. One is Carolyn Forché who is, I think, an embodiment of a tremendously important spirit of humanity and compassion, who is more frank than just about anybody else is addressing contemporary political realities—with her experience in Central America, for instance. The other writer I've been reading a great deal of lately is Raymond Carver. I came to his work through his short stories. I just read a book called *Fires* which includes a selection of his poems over the years. I find them tremendously interesting poems, tremendously moving. The poems have nothing to do really with the Midwest, although they could. We were talking before about what I admire in certain poets. Carver, I think, says it very well in the beginning of the book, in an essay called "On Writing," when he talks about what he likes and what he distrusts as a writer. He's talking specifically about fiction, but he could be talking about poetry. The kind of writing that he distrusts is the kind that seems to involve

30

trickery and gimmicks. He says, "No tricks. I hate tricks. At the first sign of a trick or gimmick in a piece of fiction, a cheap trick or even an elaborate trick, I tend to look for cover. Tricks are ultimately boring." I feel very much that way. And I think something that I find in Midwestern poetry in general, and in people we've been talking about, is an absence of tricks and gimmicks. I find a great deal of strong writing and technical skill, virtuosity. But I also find people who are communicating something that goes beyond the pyrotechnics of language and any gimmick. That's the sort of thing I would say to a young writer, the sort of thing I would say to a class on poetry.

Tammaro: Let's swing back to your own writing. I realize that you came to writing somewhat late in your life—what we might consider late—you're first book was published when you were in your thirties. You weren't writing poetry when you were an undergraduate, is that right?

Vinz: Well, I did. I did. But I was far more interested in fiction. In my undergraduate days in Kansas I took a fiction writing workshop and pretty well got knocked down because I was trying to write (I had been reading James Joyce) the "plotless" story, and my writing teachers kept pointing out to me that—as one of them wrote on one of my stories—I was "full of some fine sound and fury, signifying nothing." I'd written poems, but I didn't know what a poem was. I started writing poems in high school because I discovered Allen Ginsberg. I loved that kind of outrageousness. It went with being a teenager.

Tammaro: Who hasn't discovered Allen Ginsberg and the Beats in high school!

Vinz: Here was a guy who was saying things that I hardly dared to think! And I loved it. So I started writing in high school, you know, with some sense of being serious about it. And I knew I really wanted to go on and, if not be a writer, at least do some writing. But I kept it quiet. I think my first really serious attempt at poetry was when I was a graduate student. Ed Wolfe at the University of Kansas had a creative writing workshop and Warren Fine, who's a tremendous writer—a novelist, but in those days he was writing a lot of poetry—began intro-

31

ducing me to what a contemporary poem was. My models as an English major, as an undergraduate were Keats and Tennyson. I was really writing a 19th century, even an 18th century kind of poem. And from there I went to New Mexico and met Gene Frumkin, who was the first *real* contemporary poet I was able to talk to. And I began discovering certain things. In 1968 when I left New Mexico I was doing a lot of writing. I was getting pretty well into my twenties. I'd been writing steadily, but never doing anything—not submitting it. I was a serious graduate student and I was going to be a scholar; creative writing was just a kind of hobby. Gene was probably the first one to show me what a contemporary poem was. Gene was very heavily influenced, I think, by the Black Mountain poets and by some of the west coast poets, but he also introduced me to James Wright. The first book of poetry to simply blow me away was *The Branch Will Not Break*. It was at that point, maybe, that I decided that I really wanted to write poetry. And when I came to Moorhead I started writing more and more, and met Tom McGrath and he sort of picked up where Gene left off. And at that point, by about 1970, I started sending out my work, started getting things published. I had written for a period of probably ten years in which I really didn't ever show my work to anybody but my wife and maybe a couple of close friends.

Tammaro: Earlier you mentioned Tom McGrath. You've worked with Tom a great deal since you've been in Moorhead over the past fifteen years in a number of contexts—editor at *Dacotah Territory*, colleagues in the English Department, and doing readings together and so on. How has that been, working with Tom? Have you seen Tom's influence creeping over into your own work?

Vinz: I think I did at the beginning. Tom has a very unique sense of language. He writes in a very long line and he loves words and sounds, and his poetry is kind of supercharged. My poetry is much more understated, but I can look back at things I wrote in say 1969 or so, and I can really see a very heavy Tom McGrath influence. I can see it in the politics too. Some of the first poems I had published were poems that had to do with Viet Nam. But I think Tom's influence has been really more as a teacher. He criticized what I did. He didn't try to point me in his direction. In the early years he gave me some really solid advice. He told me some people to read. He again is a tremendously generous man, a man whose own life has been harried in many ways and yet who always has found time for young writers. As long as I've known Tom, he's always had a stack of manuscripts people have sent him.

Tammaro: One thing that I noticed in your books is that they seem to have—or perhaps maybe you seem to write poems around—a particular theme or around a particular idea or perhaps a cycle of poems. I'm thinking of *Deep Water, Dakota* and *Red River Blues,* which seem to be cohesive books. And I'm wondering: perhaps that's some of Tom's influence from his books and *Letter to An Imaginary Friend.*

Vinz: Tom and I talked about this years ago; maybe it was in the context of an interview I was doing with him. But he said he felt very fortunate on one hand, and also in a way kind of cursed, that very early in his writing career he discovered that he had a long poem in him. And everything he wrote was either a part of that long poem or what he called a "footnote" to it. He had a vision of the whole mountain which I don't think many people ever get. And I think that those talks I had with Tom probably did influence me. In my own work it seems I always have to have a sense that the poem's going to fit into something. The poems in my first collections were very heavily place-oriented and I was exploring my roots. I was exploring being a Midwesterner, so things tended to cohere around that theme. And then for several years I really put that aside and explored dreams and read the surrealist poets and explored my own dream life and reverie life. I went on from there to prose poems, and now I've been working on people poems and poems exploring the relationships between male and female. But I still write dream poems and I still write place poems. But you're right, I guess. I still have a sense of writing individual poems as part of a manuscript.

Tammaro: This is all part of that creative process—maybe a later part of the creative process. I was wondering, could you talk about your creative process? What happens in those early stages? What happens when you sit down to write? What's the role of revision in your poetry?

Vinz: First, just add a footnote to what we were saying before. I think that part of the reason for trying to see things in terms of collections or cycles has been my work as an editor, working with books, grouping poems, and doing anthologies. It's hard to escape that. It comes seeping into your work.

Tammaro: You begin to think of your own work in terms of a collection or a chapbook.

Vinz: As far as my writing process, I guess what I'd say to you would be the same kind of thing I say to a lot of my students. I am very much a streak writer. I think if I were writing a novel I would have to discipline myself to write several hours a day, as all the interviews you read say to do. I think one reason that I like poetry is that there are times that I go for quite a long stretch without really writing anything. I'll keep a journal, maybe, and my journal does not consist of any more than a couple of pages in which I just write down an image or a line or something. I think it's important always to be open to possibilities because you never know where they're going to come from. Whether it's a dream or something you see, or you go fishing and something happens—there's a poem there somewhere. We kind of joke about it, but it's very true. So I guess I try to be open to all kinds of possibilities and record something pretty constantly. But there are only specific periods when I get a chunk of time, or a quarter break, or something—then I will really immerse myself and work many hours a day writing, getting down the raw material. And then in the longer stretches of time such as a summer vacation or when I've been on sabbatical leaves, the majority of my time is spent in revision. I think it's because of being a teacher and seeing a lot of young people who come to poetry via rock music or Rod McKuen that think that poetry is simply writing down something with sincerity, and that it's just spontaneous. Yeah, there's a spontaneous element in poetry, but there's also a great deal of craft. And I guess what I have to fight with my students the most about is two things. One is reading. Where you really learn to write is through your reading. You learn what other people are doing and you learn some of the steps to take and you pick up ideas in the same way that an artist does by going to an art gallery or a musician to a concert. Again, a lot of them resist that as maybe I did once upon a time, because they don't want to be "influenced." You have to realize writers are always influenced. Everything influences the writer. The second thing is revision, realizing that a poem is probably never done, that there's always tinkering. Since I'm on a teaching schedule, I often try to finish a poem before it's really done. I've got a limited amount of time and try to force it. So I always find myself going back. Most summers I spend much more time revising than writing, going back to those things I *thought* were done—maybe even poems I'd sent out. The idea of revision is certainly far more than some of my students think, which is that it's just kind of cleaning up the manuscript.

Tammaro: Putting the commas in the right place.

Vinz: Checking the spelling. I think it was Philip Lopate who said you need to take the word very literally. Revision—re-seeing, seeing again. When you write that poem you're one person. When you come back to it, you're another person, you're different, changed. You have a different angle on things, a different perception. Maybe that original perception is going to hold up, maybe it isn't. If I have a great frustration about being a teacher of writing it is to try to convince young writers that the writing process is often mundane, and it's painful and it's time-consuming. Revision is perhaps the most important part of the writing process.

Tammaro: Bruno Bettelheim has an excellent essay on art education and the way art is taught in the schools. And he makes a similar assertion. That is, to tell young children who are working with art that self expression itself is art is really wrong. That all art is self-expression but not all self-expression is art; I've always found that as being really helpful. There are things, such as revision and hard work and there is an intensity. It's not simply journal jottings.

Vinz: I absolutely agree with that. Very, very rarely in my life have I had problems getting started with something—in poetry, anyway. I've rarely experienced what one might call writer's block. There's always something to get down. Where the real block for me has come is in the completion.

Tammaro: You have a difficulty, then, of letting go of a poem?

Vinz:	Yes.
Tammaro:	Maybe that's why books are important.
Vinz:	It's a way of saying "at least I'm going to send these out of the house."
Tammaro:	Again, a sort of a loaded question—what is a Mark Vinz poem, if there is such a creature?
Vinz:	I think there are those who will tell you it's whatever I'm working on at the moment.
Tammaro:	How would you characterize it?
Vinz:	Our mutual friend, Joe Richardson, has a definition. He calls it a "stalking" poem. And maybe he's right. I think what he means is that it's a kind of poem that may grow out of a particular place or experience that tries to move beyond itself into a kind of universal human experience. That's a very general statement, but maybe my sense of what I'm trying to do in a poem is to grasp the reader, to say, "My experience and yours aren't the same thing, but I've had this experience and if I can communicate it well, if I can find the right words, maybe it will move you, maybe you've had that kind of experience." It's what Robert Frost said—that poem will "make you remember what you didn't know you knew." I go back to the definition of poet as *vates* in Latin—"seer." That person who has a different angle on things. Not seer in the sense of prophet, but someone who sees things in a special way. And I guess that's always preoccupied me in writing poetry—to have a particular vision and yet be able, through the medium of language and certain techniques, to make that vision known to a reader, to make that reader remember something he or she didn't know they knew.
Tammaro:	Does a poem come to mind where you feel you've successfully done that?
Vinz:	Well, this is a poem I've read many times as a kind of "ars poetica." I've never written a poem directly about writing a poem. Maybe this is the closest that I've come, if you follow the metaphor. Sometimes I've written fishing poems which are really about writing poems. Writing poems and fishing are

kind of the same thing. You're putting down lines and you don't know what you're going to come up with. This is a poem I wrote several years ago. It's called "Processional." It's about a particular experience, walking with my daughter, walking our dog, and her discovery that she and the dog were the same age. But that the dog was really very old, and my daughter was very young. That was sort of the point that the poem turned on, and from that it catapulted me back into my own childhood. So anyway, I'll read the poem. It's called "Processional."

> You and your child go out
> to walk the dog—
> like two dark ponies they bound ahead
> then wait to see if you will follow patiently.
> By calendars they are the same age now,
> though you have read somewhere
> that dog years count for more—
> she's closer to your parents' age than yours.
>
> You walk the dog,
> who sniffs the dying grass in frantic loops
> while you bury noses deep inside your coats
> and watch the Dipper filling up with frosty breath.
> Under every streetlight now
> you skip across the sidewalk cracks—
> still afraid to break some mother's back.
>
> Too long, too late, you walk the dog,
> three generations wondering:
> why winter comes so soon this year,
> the shooting star that drops into the trees,
> and how to skip across those cracks
> you cannot see.

Maybe that's my idea of writing a poem; it's skipping across those cracks—the ones you see, but more importantly, the ones you don't see, that through metaphor or through some other kind of hinting you can touch on. And if it's a good poem, something opens up for you then. And for the reader.

Tammaro: Frost talks about the way you look at a star, and if you tilt your head a certain way it just sort of glistens or glimmers with a certain kind of light. So we all may be looking at the same star, but only those who tilt their heads that certain way will see that certain glimmer.

Vinz: The problem is, I think—this is the teacher side of me coming out—getting people to look. Too many people say, "Poetry, I can't understand that, I won't read it" and so on. And I found again and again in my classes and in the Writers-in-the-Schools program, once you get them to take that look, they find that it's nothing like they imagined it to be at all. It's interesting we have so many hang-ups when it comes to poetry. We as a culture, I mean. And yet if you look at poetry as that sense of learning a new way to see, and that seeing ultimately is looking inside yourself, the poem becomes the medium for doing that.

Tammaro: Maybe this goes back to what you were saying when you left Kansas to go out to New Mexico and you met Gene Frumkin. He was the first person who told you or showed you what a contemporary poem was. And he began to teach you how to see. I think I've had similar kinds of experiences. I've seen that—in other people—that poetry, that writing as a way of life is a valid way of life, a way of living. And I think that happened to me at a very young age, at 17 or 18 years old. I saw people who had made the commitment to live that way. And I felt, "Yes, I affirm that."

Vinz: I think that's very important, and if I look back at the way poems were taught to me when I was in school, there was none of that. They were always too remote, or taught simply in technical terms, and that *seeing* was never allowed to take place.

Tammaro: You got the sense that the poems you were reading in a book were written for the book that you were reading because it was going to be for that class that someone was going to teach. That's the concept I always had. Someone was producing the poems because they had to be in this book that was eventually going to be taught. Not that poetry came out of a life.

Vinz: The way poetry was taught to me was as a math equation. It was something to be solved. Something that existed for its own sake and for your status in that course. But even thinking

38

back to elementary school, poems were always taught that way. They were cryptic things and the teacher knew the answer; nobody else did. It had nothing to do with life or experience.

Tammaro: I wonder how much of that resulted from the heavy influence that New Critics had in separating the life of the poet from the poem as a way of trying to talk intelligently about the poetry. Eventually, we separated the writer from the poem.

Vinz: It certainly hit me in graduate school and I think I've spent a good deal in the last few years unlearning many of the things I learned in graduate school.

Tammaro: On this subject of teaching: you've been teaching creative writing for many, many years and a lot of students have passed through your classrooms. How do you work in class? How do you teach creative writing? If you were printing a little pamphlet about teaching creative writing, what would your pamphlet contain? I'm thinking of Dick Hugo's book called *The Triggering Town* full of wonderful essays.

Vinz: The first thing I do is to spend some time talking about and reading poems, and then ask the students about their commitment to poetry and what a poem is, and why they want to write poems. Is it simply to record a spontaneous feeling, or is something more than that? What is their commitment to language? At the beginning, I just try to show them some models. I try to throw a lot of material at them to get them reading. I guess that's the first step. If you're teaching an introductory course, some of them really do need exercises. I'm really skeptical of exercises. But sometimes they can generate some pretty interesting stuff. I try to be honest with the students. I've been saying, "I'll give you some exercises. This may or may not result in anything, but they're good things to try as long as you can realize the difference between an exercise and the real thing." At the same time, I'm really encouraging them to keep journals, to look at their journals as repositories, as places to experiment, to write things in different ways, to revise. And I guess beyond that, what I try to do is really put them in a workshop situation as soon as I possibly can, even in the introductory courses. The upper division courses I teach are 90 percent workshop situations where I get them critiquing each others' work, because that's when they really learn about their own work. I try to get a positive exchange going, which a lot of times is very hard to do with poetry writers. I don't have any problems with fiction writers—they tend to be much more workmanlike. Everybody knows what a story is, and a plot, and character. The ground rules are much clearer. Poetry is much more subjective and I think individual personalities and individual passions sometimes stand in the way. And while I don't think I've ever had tears in a fiction writing class, they come pretty often in a poetry class. Especially in an upper division course, I want them to read their work aloud. I want them to give and receive serious criticism and to take it seriously. I think all the talking that I do and all the exercises and all the things that I have them read perhaps aren't as valuable as reaching that stage when they actually can read and react and exchange and revise as a result of that. So my emphasis has very much been on the workshop, even for beginning students.

Tammaro: So what you're talking about, then, gathering and agreeing that, "Hey, we're writers and we're going to think and talk as writers, and we're going to engage in a high level of imagination and give attention to the poems," and get them thinking as writers, which for many of them probably has never happened in their lives. And maybe they have for the first time in their lives someone who is thinking and talking seriously and intelligently about their writing. For me that was a really important experience. And again, I go back to that idea when I began to think that "Yes, writing is a way of life; poetry is a way of life."

Vinz: I suppose to be honest, in my students—and I'm sure this is true all over—there's a very small percentage of them that are going to really go on with it. But I want to introduce them to the facts so that they don't string themselves along. If you want to write for yourself, that's fine. If you don't, then you should know these things. Some of them, I'm sure, come out of my classes and say, "Well, that's it. I'm going to write only for myself." But at least they can make those choices.

Tammaro: I always think of writing in terms of other arts, and think, for example, of photography, and say, "If you want to stay at the level of Kodak Instamatic, or if you want to move up to maybe 35 mm. and then if you want to move up to the Hassleblad. And then do your own developing instead of sending it out. This is an art, this is a discipline, and that as much as you want to engage your mind and your imagination, the discipline will allow you to do so.

Vinz: The metaphor I use is very similar, but it's from music. You don't sit down at a piano and expect to play a concerto the first time. You learn scales. You learn the techniques. And once you get through that...for a lot of students, that's the breaking point. Once they realize this is serious stuff, they don't want to learn those techniques. In my last ten years of teaching creative writing, I think maybe there were seven or eight students—most of them have gone on to graduate school—who were truly smitten. And you can tell—the ones that are possessed.

Tammaro: How do you work with that individual writer, when you do recognize him or her, or when the student recognizes it, and then you recognize that the student has recognized it. That's an important crossroad. Where do you go from there?

Vinz: Well, quite often, if that's the case, the student is not getting a whole lot out of the workshop because he or she happens to be just that far ahead of the other students. Although, in my experience, most of those students still value the workshop because they're getting criticism at one level or another. I guess I try to work with them at that point much more independently. I try to introduce them to other writers. I try to get them involved with some writers who aren't students so they can meet them and learn from them in a direct kind of way. We've been fortunate here that there's always been a community of writers in which that can happen. At that point, too, I guess I really encourage them to submit their work. I do *not* encourage young writers to submit their work. I've known writing teachers who make it a requirement of a writing class that they all send off their work. In fact, I *received* many of those poems when I was editing. And I think that if a student really wants to, then you tell that student what submitting means, what to expect, what a form rejection slip means. But most of them

42

aren't ready to submit, nor should they be encouraged to submit. The really good student should, because that after all is the other real test—one has to send one's work out beyond the workshop, beyond the teacher to get their response of that editor far away.

Tammaro: How does all of that affect your own writing? You're in there looking at other people's writing and talking at this high level about writing and suddenly you go home and say, "Now, maybe I'll lower my standards a little bit for my own writing."

Vinz: I came across an interview with John Barth years ago where the interviewer had asked him that question, I think expecting to find that there was a one-to-one correlation, that working with all of these talented young people would have a positive effect on Barth's work. Barth's answer is one that I've used many times: "It delays its completion." If you're working in an atmosphere where writing is happening and you're talking over writing and you're reading, sharing, and reacting, it can't help but influence your work. But in my case, only in the most general sort of sense.

Tammaro: And along with those lines, what about when you're in the classroom teaching literature and then you go home to write the poem.

Vinz: On a general level, there's an influence there, but very rarely on a specific level.

Tammaro: From January, 1971 to December of '82 you published 17 issues of *Dacotah Territory* and 15 chapbooks and books. And then you ended *Dacotah Territory* in '82. In 1983 you had two major collections: *Climbing the Stairs* from Spoon River Poetry Press and *The Weird Kid* from New Rivers Press. I was wondering if there's any correlation between cutting ties with *Dacotah Territory* and the proliferation of your own work—getting back to your own work after all those years of editing.

Vinz: I think there's not a direct connection in that. Most of the poems in both collections were written during the years that I edited *Dacotah Territory*. I think ending *Dacotah Territory* and having a sabbatical gave me time finally to go back and revise

43

and finish and write the poems I needed to complete the collections. I had done the magazine for ten years, a great deal of it by myself. I had had help from time to time, but the work simply took a great deal out of me and it was one more thing to take away from my writing. Giving up the magazine was something that I felt I had to do. I'd burned out on it. Ten years seemed like a good round number, and The North Dakota Institute for Regional Studies had agreed to publish a ten year retrospective anthology and I thought that was a nice way to end it. The sort of deal I made with myself was that I would take a few years off from any small press activity and reassess. And if I ever start again I don't think I'd do a magazine. I would do something more manageable—perhaps a series of chapbooks, or an anthology, both of which I am doing now!

Tammaro: Let's stay on that topic of *Dacotah Territory*. I want to read you a couple of things that I pulled out from the early issues. In issue #2, for example, you wrote that one of the goals of *Dacotah Territory* was—and I'll quote you—"to tap into the poetry of place flourishing around us, but never to be simply limited by it. To take a stand against the placelessness of American society, but not with down-homism." And then from the first advertising flyer for *Dacotah Territory*, again I'll quote: "We see ourselves then as importers and exporters seeking the best work from both the new and established writers no matter what their place, that unique vitality which partakes of both the local and international simultaneously." So the question: to what degree do you think *Dacotah Territory* succeeded in achieving those goals that you were setting for yourself?

Vinz: As I think about *Dacotah Territory*'s successes and failures, that's probably the one thing I feel the best about. I think we really were able to maintain that balance. You'll find issues that prove exceptions, but if you look at what we published over the ten years you'll find a very good blend of people from the Midwest, people from outside, different varieties of writing, different techniques, even to some extent different schools. I think at the same time, the magazine did tend to cohere around a certain kind of writing. And we did tend to publish more Midwesterners than not. That was the idea of import/ export. It was *not* a magazine simply to promote Midwestern writers although that was an important aim of the magazines.

44

But it's also good for Midwestern writers to know what's going on in other parts of the country.

Tammaro: At its peak, how many people were subscribing to *Dacotah Territory* including libraries and so on?

Vinz: I can't remember those figures offhand, but I would say we did a print run of about a thousand and we pretty well sold out each issue. Some of those would be contributors' copies, so a few hundred subscriptions and some to bookstores. But there were not many distributors in those days.

Tammaro: Was that a surprise to you? After four or five years were you really pleased with that or were you feeling as though there could be more people out there who would want to subscribe. Were you pleased with that?

Vinz: I was pleased, but more subscribers also meant more work for me, since *editing* a magazine is perhaps only 10 percent of the real work. You know, all the mailing and bookkeeping and corresponding is the bulk of the work. I felt very comfortable that we were getting around. I was getting responses from all over the country, even a kind of national recognition. And at the same time it was manageable. It was really at the limits of what I could do. As many people have said, doing a little magazine is a "labor of love." But it was testing my love.

Tammaro: So over all, you feel as though the experiment worked, and you have no qualms about it, no regrets. You might even do it again perhaps.

Vinz: I don't know that I'd ever do it again because I'll never be as young as I was then. I'll never have the kind of energy and zeal again. But it was very rewarding in the sense of putting me in contact with some of the people we've already talked about, and building some friendships, and introducing me to writing that influenced me—that sense of the community, of discovering the Midwest was tied into my own writing. There are important side benefits in doing a magazine!

Tammaro: Let's say that a year from now you were going to do another magazine similar to *Dacotah Territory*. What would you do differently as a result of having done *Dacotah Territory* for ten years?

Vinz: One thing I would do differently: before I started, I would try to establish funding. We were lucky as a little magazine. We were able to sell a lot, and over the years maybe only 30 percent of our budget came from grant money. Still, a great deal of time was burned up looking for that money and wondering whether there would be money to pay the printer and so on. I really would want to find a way to establish a kind of consistent financial solvency.

Tammaro: Underwrite the magazine for three years or something like that and let it...

Vinz: That would be handy. I also wouldn't do it without help; I really would want more assistance—Grayce Ray was a wonderful associate, but there was still more work than we could handle. In our last couple of issues we went to a yearly thematic anthology simply because I did not have the wherewithal in terms of my own resources, spiritually or financially, to bring out two issues a year, or three, as we did once upon a time. So we decided to do one issue annually and to center on a theme. *Dacotah Territory 16* was hotel and cafe poems and photographs and 17 was Fathers—poems by, for, and about fathers. I liked that angle. Nobody else seemed to be doing that. Finally, something that always discourages me a little bit as an editor is to look at magazines and see a great deal of sameness. The same people, the same kind of poems—magazines that don't really seem to have any particular reason for existing. I always felt that *Dacotah Territory* did. Maybe it was our Midwestern bias. If I were to think again about doing a magazine, I would really want to find and establish another good reason for its existing.

Tammaro: Many times—and I've heard this comment from a number of people—when talking about small presses, they talk about how much they like chapbooks because they're small and efficient and economical and they're usually much more focused than a large book that is 48 or 64 pages. And I was wondering if you ever—not that *Dacotah Territory* was ever guilty of that—but did you ever feel as though sometimes you were just trying to fill out your commitment to the page numbers?

Vinz:	Maybe in some of the early issues, but certainly not in the later issues.
Tammaro:	By then you were getting enough quality material?
Vinz:	We were getting so much we were holding more and more and more. We were doing double issues to catch up. So, I always was very fortunate as an editor, and I don't know why—just the breaks I guess. I found that I had a lot of good material.
Tammaro:	How long did that take to happen from the first issue in '71 to the point where you had the overflow basket and you were backed up for an issue?
Vinz:	I think it happened with number 6, which we did in 1973. Jim White had lived with the Navajo and had many ties to the Native American community, and I was very interested in certain Native American writers. So, I asked Jim if he would put together a Native American issue. John Milton had done one for *South Dakota Review* and I was impressed with his work. And so, Jim did, and we were fortunate the National Endowment Literature Program, through Leonard Randolph, got very interested. The National Endowment bought 2,000 copies at cost and distributed them to every state arts agency in the country.
Tammaro:	What was the name of that issue?
Vinz:	It was just called a Special Native American Issue. And as a result of that, *Dacotah Territory* got very well known and I think with those ensuing issues—7, 8, 9 and on, that's when all of a sudden manuscripts were coming in from all over because people had seen the Native American issue and had liked it. Also, as a result of that, two years later we did a follow up Native American anthology, this time not as an issue of the magazine, as I'd originally intended, because we were too full. So we did the second collection, which was called *The First Skin Around Me*, as a book.
Tammaro:	I hear you saying this a number of times throughout the conversation about diversity and the importance of diversity and that's something you see in American poetry. In addition to that, what else did you learn about contemporary American poetry as an editor? What were you learning, what were you

seeing, or feeling about contemporary American poetry? Obviously you read lots of manuscripts over the ten years and corresponded with many writers.

Vinz: On the negative side, I found a great deal of sameness. Certain people have written something called "Little Magazine Verse." You don't find it anywhere else. It's formulaic sort of verse. I'd have a hard time defining it, but I did find a great deal of sameness. I did find a great deal of posing. We talked about that before. I tried to deal with that in *Letters to the Poetry Editor*. It's very sad in some ways to be an editor because when you read those letters that come in there is often such a desperation to be published, anywhere, at any cost. And that, I found very discouraging. On the other hand, I consistently found new writers that surprised me, writers I entered into correspondence with, writers who went on to have books. It was a great joy for me to sign the copyright releases and to keep track of them. So I found two things: one—something that was very deadening and repetitious, but just as much on the other side, I found a lot of fresh, interesting, and exciting work coming from the Midwest, but also coming from Canada, and coming from many parts of the United States. I think the only part of the country that I heard very little from was the South. We never got very many submissions from there.

Tammaro: You think the name may have frightened some people away?

Vinz: I don't know. I've wondered about that!

Tammaro: Can you identify a couple of the real pleasures or real joys during the ten years? Maybe publishing someone's chapbook or a poem by a young poet?

Vinz: Well, I would say the chapbook series in general. Because I think as we found the magazine was becoming national in scope and we were publishing as many writers from outside the Midwest as in the Midwest, I felt a way to kind of restore that commitment we talked about a little bit ago—the import/ export idea—would be to look seriously at some very talented, younger writers within my own region. And one of the things that led me to found *Dacotah Territory* with some students at Moorhead State was that we began to discover a tremendous, flourishing writing community in our own area. It was work

48

that we wanted to print, we wanted to send out, we wanted to recognize. The first chapbook, done in '73, was by Jim Fawbush, who had been a student of mine. He had done a collection of poems, I believe, as kind of an honors thesis. And one of Grayce's friends happened to be taking a typesetting course and she needed a project, so that was how the chapbook was born. I had paper left over from issues of *Dacotah Territory*. We had free letter-press typesetting, and we had the manuscript. And lo and behold, we had a chapbook series! We went on to publish collections by Michael Moos, Dale Jacobson, Bob Waldridge, and David Martinson, all former students; Grayce Ray, my associate editor; Mary Pryor, a colleague in the English department; and Tony Oldknow, Dick Lyons, and Dave Solheim, all of whom had been associated with North Dakota State University. These last five were older people— who had been writing poems for several years. So the chapbook series also had a kind of age diversity.

Tammaro: I'm hearing something that reflects some of my experiences. One of the other bonuses when you're involved in small presses is that making a book tends to be a cooperative spirit, that authors are very much involved—sometimes as much as they want or as little as they want. But there tends to be involvement by a number of people in the making of chapbooks and books. Often you don't get that when you hit it with a larger publisher. You hand over the poems and something happens over there that you're not quite sure happens and the galleys come back. But in small press you have people—artists, typesetters, and printer friends, and so on. And there is that sense of community and cooperation. It sounds as though you have experienced some of that in putting together the chapbooks.

Vinz: Very much so. And since all the people were within the region, there was direct contact. It wasn't by mail. It was sitting down and hashing it over—should this poem be here or should this poem be there? Should we use this poem? I learned a lot about being an editor doing the chapbooks, making those kinds of decisions, and Grayce did too.

Tammaro: Well, in 1975 you, along with Joe Richardson, established and pioneered one of the unique literary ventures to come along in a long time, *Plains Distribution Service*. At the time, it was a revolutionary idea and since then has not been duplicated, but certainly has been a model for other kinds of distribution agencies. When I think of distribution I always think of *Plains Distribution* and that crazy Book Bus rolling across the Midwest! I don't want to turn this into a retrospective, but how do you feel about it—with 20-20 hindsight?

Vinz: Mainly, I feel very proud of it. I think it's one of the most worthwhile things I've been involved with. *Plains* was one of those fortunate circumstances. As I was doing the first issue of *Dacotah Territory*, I met Joe Richardson, who was managing a bookstore, and we talked about publishing—he asked me what the main problems were with small press, and in those days— and to some extent now—the main problem was distribution. He had some good ideas. We eventually went to the National Endowment for the Arts and got a grant and put together our first booklists and our reading committee. His vision and mine were very similar, but he had strength that I didn't. He had tremendous organizational and business sense. He didn't know much about poetry or literature except that he liked it. So the two of us were able to parlay *Plains*, through one means or another, into a growing concern that helped a great deal of people. It brought people together. We were able to bring our magazine committee to Fargo for a Midwest Editors' Meeting. We had even a national distributors meeting here. We also published quarterly booklists screened and selected by our board and by our reading committee. The book bus toured the five states plus Upper Michigan and Nebraska. We sponsored somewhere around 300 readings and workshops. So there was a lot of exposure for writers, money going back to writers and presses. We had several other projects that were only in the developing stages when the funding disappeared in about 1980. But we had five very strong years and we accomplished a lot, and I think that that is certainly much more due to Joe Richardson than to me. And also to our board and to our staff people, and to my wife, Betsy, who was involved a great deal in *Plains*.

Tammaro: Again, it sounds like a cooperative effort, and we keep hitting on that, it keeps surfacing. And maybe that's characteristic of what it's like to be involved or engaged in the state of literature here in the Midwest.

50

Vinz: It has been a kind of community since the beginnings of small press, back to *Poetry* magazine in 1912. There's been that sense of a lot of people really pulling together. On other levels of publishing you see a great deal more competition. I'm not saying it doesn't exist in small press; certainly within small press there are people who are far more interested in marketing than in editing. That's one of the discouraging things to me. But by and large there is a sense of community, a sense of pulling together.

Tammaro: Well, you're someone who's been actively engaged in the small press world for many years. What are you seeing now that you didn't see maybe eight or ten years ago in that world? Are you seeing things that have changed for the better or have things gotten worse? There's probably both sides to that issue there.

Vinz: For one thing, I see more magazines—not always that we need more. But when I started *Dacotah Territory* in the early '70s there were very, very few magazines in Minnesota and certainly few in the Upper Midwest. Now I see several, and I think that those of us who went on before helped make those things possible. That's a very positive kind of change, although not all of those magazines really have demonstrated a very clear need for existence. I still see that very strong sense of community. I also see the continuing existence of Bookslinger, a very good small press distributor. And I see some of the ideas that started with *Plains* and other distributors in the 70s really being carried through now by other people. For example, we were very interested in syndication—in syndicating fiction and poetry to newspapers. We were simply never able to bring that off, although we did a very useful study and turned that material over to the National Endowment. Now, the National Endowment funds the PEN Fiction Syndication Project. That's a very good feeling to think something that we worked on several years ago is now coming to fruition.

Tammaro: Many people would say that increase of money during the past decades from the National Endowment for the Arts has caused a lot of mixed reactions: you have X number of presses competing for Y number of dollars. And that tends to set up a kind of competition so you have a sort of small press horse race. Greg

51

Kuzma writes articulately about the influences of government funding on literature and art. And certainly Robert Bly also has voiced *his* concern that perhaps government support of the arts may be a downfall of small presses and contemporary literature.

Vinz: I don't know if it's a downfall, but it certainly is a danger. I think if money's available, there's a temptation to go after it even if you don't have a very good reason for doing it. And that has caused some dissension. As small presses grow, every issue of *The International Directory of Small Presses and Little Magazines* gets 50 pages bigger each year. The bigger something becomes, the more splits, and the more politicking are bound to happen. But I say by and large, small press remains much healthier than large, commercial publishers who are very limited in what they can publish.

Tammaro: What do you think is needed these days in small press?

Vinz: I think small presses' greatest lack is criticism. We need serious criticism. We need journals to expand their review pages. I would like to see more serious small press reviews, and perhaps in the form of critical journals. If you look at the major review media in this country, they're very clearly weighted toward the large publishing houses on either coast. Even writers publishing with some of the bigger Midwestern university presses sometimes have a hard time getting reviewed.

Tammaro: *Library Journal* every November-December had what is called "Small Press Roundup," like get the cattle together for branding or something like that. I feel as though it was their token nod or acknowledgement of small press. And one wonders why couldn't they expand their biweekly columns to include small press? And getting books into libraries. That's another important area. I've talked to a number of writers and editors and they always feel that they have a very hard time selling to libraries.

Vinz: To get those library sales you need some kind of legitimizing agent, and that is the review. And more than the review, the serious critical article.

Tammaro: Your last book published in 1983 was a book called *The Weird*

Kid—one of the winners of the 1983 Minnesota Voices Competition, sponsored by New Rivers Press and published by New Rivers Press. That was a book of prose poems which obviously is a very different kind of direction for you in terms of the kind of poem that you've been writing. And then recently you had two of your stories accepted for the NEA Fiction Syndication Project. I was wondering of the relationship between the prose poem and your stepping into fiction.

Vinz: Well, two reasons. One is I've been always very interested in fiction. I started writing fiction and even all the years I was writing pretty much exclusively poetry, I would be scratching out a story or writing down ideas for stories. And in the late '70s I found that my poems were becoming, it seemed to me, increasingly prosaic. I was losing interest in the lyricism of the line. About this time I started reading prose poems. Greg Kuzma had done a nice collection from *Pebble*, and Robert Bly had also done a lot of work with prose poems. I picked up Michael Benedikt's anthology from Dell, *The Prose Poem*. It was a whole new world. It was also kind of a lark. I started experimenting and found that it kind of relieved that pressure that was building up in me that wanted to tell stories and be prosaic. The other thing, something that Bly talks about, is that the prose poem is very much more open-ended to imagination, to association. If you read some of Bly—especially his early prose poems—they're often loose, sprawling collections of associations of "leaping" images.

Tammaro: *The Morning Glory* collection.

Vinz: Yes, for one. And since I had been working on dream poems, I was very much interested in the kind of associative leaps that can come about from reverie. So prose poems opened up access to a whole different direction. I could bring in character and plot and certain elements of fiction, I could dabble in surrealism, and so on.

Tammaro: So you worked with the prose poem. In *The Weird Kid* there are forty-four poems, and I was curious as to whether those poems were written in one of those streaks that you talked about earlier. I guess I'm curious about the writing of the book and what you discovered about the form of the prose poem.

Vinz: I did write a number of them—probably half of that manuscript that survived—in one summer in a tremendous streak. I think it's very hard to define what a prose poem is. Everybody has a slightly different definition. It's a hybrid—some prose poems are more like poetry in prose form in that they work through metaphor and imaginative leaps and so on. Other prose poems, it seems to me, are more like fiction, going, let's say, in the direction of somebody like Russel Edson. They tend to have character, plot, setting: they're really minimalist short stories. I have a short story anthology of contemporary fiction that categorizes some of the experimental forms of fiction, and the last one is called "Minimalist Fiction," and what they are is prose poems. The prose poems in that anthology also appeared in a poetry anthology! So nobody, I think, quite knows. I think that's the thing that excited me the most about prose poems: everybody who writes them re-invents the form for himself or herself. In *The Weird Kid*, some of them are dialogues, some of them are more like stories, some of them are more like poems. I was finding my "regular" poetry was getting more and more somber and serious and I think that the prose poems gave me a chance to be satirical and whimsical and sometimes downright silly. And I enjoyed that too.

Tammaro: Do you have a favorite of one of those that does what you want the prose poem to do?

Vinz: I think my favorite is the title poem, "The Weird Kid." It was the first that I really felt satisfied with, although it went through two or three different versions. It was tied into my own memory of a kind of person that I think is archetypal in many people's experience. It wasn't an essay, it wasn't a vignette, it wasn't a story, it wasn't a poem. It was this *thing*, and it never would have been written had I not said, "I'm going to write a prose poem." And so that, I guess, remains my favorite.

Tammaro: What in a poem didn't allow you to do what you could do in *The Weird Kid*; what was preventing you from doing what you did?

Vinz: Too much of an interest in the line and in the form of the

54

poem—the formal aspects.

Tammaro: I suspect that when you read that at readings people begin to see a little bit of the weird kid in themselves, and it's probably a good chuckle, a good poem to have to break up the intensity of a reading.

Vinz: It's frequently the poem I end with. A lot of the readings I've given I will end—partly because it's been my most recent book—with a few prose poems because they're very different from the other kinds I've read. But I always end with that one because it's an upper. It's also a very serious poem. And it's a poem that will provoke responses. And I think people who have been to my readings or have read "The Weird Kid" have probably responded more positively to that poem than to anything else I've ever written. Maybe it's because of the universality of the "Charlies" in our lives or the fact that, as you say, that weird kid is a part of all of us. Some of us deal with that part frankly, some of us suppress it. I see that in my own children, especially as teenagers. It's very hard to laugh at yourself at that age. It takes a bit more distance and a few more years before that really can happen.

Tammaro: In 1983 you turned from the prose poem form and veered into the short story with some degree of success: the first stories were accepted for the NEA Syndication Project and another was published in the *Colorado State Review*. How are you finding the short story venture?

Vinz: It's a lark and I'm loving it! As I've said before, when I was writing prose poems I was trying to write stories. I was trying to take some of the prose poems and string them together and turn them into stories. I finally turned back to stories after not having written stories for quite a long time. And I found that I enjoyed that tremendously. It was an alternative to poetry. I liked the going back and forth. If I'm working on a poem I have a hard time writing a story, and vice versa. But the story form tested other parts of me and afforded me other kinds of opportunities. I was on sabbatical leave during part of 1982 and 1983, and during that time I wrote somewhere between fifteen and twenty stories. I didn't write very many poems during that period.

55

Tammaro: I hope they didn't take your sabbatical away because you wrote short stories instead of poems!

Vinz: No. I had said on my application for sabbatical that I was going to finish a poetry manuscript, but that also I wanted to write fiction. So I didn't lie to them. I'm finding now, in going back, that a lot of those stories I was so happy with a year ago or two years ago are ones that really aren't anywhere near being completed. I look at them, I suppose, really, as extended journal entries. And I'm trying to develop the kind of discipline that a fiction writer needs. Not to say that a poet isn't disciplined, but it's a different kind. The fiction writer has to have a daily discipline. So I find that it's hard to write short stories unless I have the time. My leave afforded me that, and these past few summers I've been doing a lot of work on fiction. I find it really hard to do much work on fiction and try to teach full time and do the other things that I do.

Tammaro: You need those blocks of time in order to sustain yourself through it.

Vinz: What I have right now in my notebooks are probably five or six stories, some of which are simply outlines, some of which are partial drafts. And I just haven't found time to go back and do that methodical kind of work to get those stories where I want them.

Tammaro: Are you finding the subject matter in those stories different from the concerns or themes that you find in your poems? Has fiction allowed you to explore different territory?

Vinz: I think that's why I said before that it was a lark. It really is, venturing out into very new territory. And I think, as with the prose poems, it's afforded me a way to use my imagination that I didn't have before. Sometimes my stories are about, you know, a husband and a wife who get into a particular situation and perhaps it's a kind of situation that I've been in with my wife. It's a situation that we've resolved completely, but in my imagination I say, "What would happen if somebody very much like me were in that situation, and it were resolved in a different way?" So I write kind of an alternative scenario, just to see what happens. That is a great deal of fun. Sometimes my stories get to be very depressing because some of those scenarios lead into some very dark waters, and that happens with poems too. But a poem is a short "take," whereas a story is a more involved working out, or working through.

Tammaro: I'm thinking of an interview with Raymond Carver in *The Paris Review*. He comments that "the fiction I'm most interested in has lines of reference to the real world" and he says, "None of my stories really happened, of course, but there's always something, some element, something said to me of that I witnessed or that may be the starting place." And that sounds similar to what you're saying. That may not be something that's a terribly new discovery, or insightful about it, but it's certainly the way it happens.

Vinz: It's been a new discovery! Or maybe it's something that I've known intellectually for a long time, but to really re-learn it intuitively and practically is another matter altogether.

Tammaro: The interviewer also asks Carver if he ever felt that alcohol was in any way an inspiration, and he mentions the poem "Vodka" that was published in *Esquire* and Carver says, "My God, no. I hope I made that clear." And I think there's that sense of "just because things happen in my fiction, does not necessarily mean that they've happened in my life." And I think that especially in young writers that happens. And I'm sure that you run into that a great deal where there's almost a transcription of literal experience—it's transcription, but it's not transformation.

Vinz: Right. I have to argue with my students constantly to expand, to change, and they say, "Oh, that's not the way it happened." But I say, "No, fiction *isn't* the way it happened." It's a variation of that.

Tammaro: You know, looking back at a couple of your earlier books, I'm struck by the nature of how sometimes they tend to really hang together and be very coherent books centered on a particular theme or idea. For example, in *Deep Water, Dakota*, there are characters from a specific place. It was a specific time and there were specific characters. And that's very fictional. That was a fictional place, obviously. And so those elements of fiction were really working there in those poems and maybe you weren't aware of it as much as perhaps you are now, working

57

	in the realm of fiction.
Vinz:	I think that's a good observation.
Tammaro:	I'm thinking, too, of *Songs For a Hometown Boy*, again a specific place, an unmentioned place, but a very specific place with specific characters, an homage to the lost souls out there who for one reason or another get distracted in their lives in some Midwestern town. And that's certainly, on one scale, very fictional, so maybe it doesn't surprise me or maybe it doesn't surprise you, then, that fiction would eventually become a part of your writing.
Vinz:	What you say is very true, and maybe I didn't recognize it at the time, but during that period I found more of a need to write poem sequences that were tied to a particular place with particular characters or recurring themes. I guess maybe that was the kind of prologue to going back to fiction writing. You mentioned Raymond Carver. It always strikes me that his stories were written in much the same way his poems were. He's an intuitive kind of writer, and I think I am too. When you start writing a story, you start with a certain kind of premise, or perhaps a character, or perhaps nothing more than a line. You never know quite where it's going to take you. What's happened to you the day before yesterday is probably going to get into your story. That's something I find very exciting about writing fiction, at least the kind of fiction I've been working on. It allows a great deal of room for that kind of following all of your intuitive bents. Many fiction writers are far more methodical. They will think through a story and plot it out and graph it and plan it. I think that Carver, in his interviews and his essays, says he's not that kind of fiction writer. He follows his inclinations; he never quite knows where a story is going to go. I don't either. And to me that is the single most exciting thing about both poetry and fiction, I *don't* know! That to me is the point where poetry and fiction come together.
Tammaro:	So finally, it's not so much the form that the thought takes; it's the thought that's expressed. The whole process then becomes important. I have a friend who once said that maybe we concern ourselves too much with the form that writing should take, and maybe we should just concern ourselves with the

best form for us. And whether we call it poetry, essay, journal writing, or short story may be secondary or peripheral to the matter at heart.

Vinz: You know, I agree with that in large part, and maybe that's where the prose poems and the short stories have taken me. And perhaps they've taken me back kind of full circle to look at my poems in a different light. I'm not sure. Perhaps my poems are a bit more open-ended now than they were once. Maybe the most important difference, on the other hand, is how one uses autobiography. One can use bits and pieces of autobiography in fiction, but if you read most fiction writers' autobiographically you will really get into trouble. As I said, if you read my stories autobiographically you will think that I am a tremendously screwed-up, unhappy person, which is not the case. I think there's a much more direct autobiographical link in my experience with the poetry—more immediate expression of something I've seen or felt, where I'm talking more as *me*. Not that I'm a confessional poet—I really am not. But I'm taking more out of my whole self in a poem than I am in a story. A story to me is a mosaic. There are parts of me in it, but there are parts of other things, too. And as I said, there are a lot of speculative things and alternatives, and alternative scenarios. So there's an important similarity, but also a very important difference.

Tammaro: What about some of your new manuscripts? You shared some of those with me and I'm recognizing some new areas that you're getting into. You mentioned earlier about exploring male/female relationships. In the one manuscript I see some concerns with grief and suffering that were not as dominant or prevalent in some of your other books. Are these all new areas for you?

Vinz: I think so. In the new book, *Mixed Blessings*, I've just been reworking, the poems are all people-oriented; many are poems about people in my family—my grandfather, or my father, my mother. But also there are also some poems that are about people that are written more as case studies, from a kind of distance. That's a theme of dealing with death, perhaps. In that collection, I probably looked more squarely at death than I ever have before, which is no doubt related to my father's dying.

And I found that to be a tremendous challenge. Other poems in the collection, which is only beginning to take shape, turn around male/female relationships. Maybe that's something that carried from my stories back to my poetry. I'm trying to cover ground from childhood, to people I know, to things that have happened, and things that I've observed revolving around maleness, especially—how maleness gets defined from the time we're children. All those false aspects of maleness that we have to live with and that some of us never lose, that some of us try to confront and change, and may resent. Anyway, I've also—as you well know, since you're its editor—put together another collection, called *Minnesota Gothic*—a return to poetry of place, but with, as the title suggests, a different kind of emphasis than in most of my earlier place-oriented poems. And, aside from working to shape and revise a collection of short stories, I've also finished preliminary work on a new collection of prose poems called *Late Night Calls* —a kind of "Son of *Weird Kid*" I suppose.

Tammaro: In your stories and poems, do you have much sense of an audience when you're writing? Is the audience for poems the same audience for stories? Some writers have specific, ideal audiences. Who is your audience?

Vinz: It's probably the same audience for both fiction and poetry. One of the things I'm interested in as a writer is the idea of accessibility. Again, I go back to a writer like Raymond Carver, who says, "Sometimes there gets to be a rather insane emphasis in contemporary writing on technique, a technique that you can admire from a distance technically, but doesn't move you." Sort of innovation for its own sake. I've always been very concerned about that. I want to reach people on some level. I want to communicate something. Writing is certainly a craft, something that you spend your life as a writer learning. But I don't think that we as writers can ever really lose touch with the idea that writing is ultimately a form of communication. It may not be communicating an idea or theme. It may be a feeling, it may be a bit of whimsy, or your particular "take" on a situation. A sort of parallel to that is the idea that I see quite often in students: working to get over privacy. If I'm writing about falling in love, that's my love experience; it's private with me. But in a poem or a story it has to be something more than that. There's a difference between being private and being personal. When a writer writes, he or she is really two people. One is the private individual and the other is the representative human being. It's *your* love experience and yet everybody falls in love, so we write at that point where our lives cross everybody's lives. And that's accessibility in my definition. It's what I've been involved with for the last twenty years. Plains Distribution was involved with making poetry accessible to an audience that may not necessarily want to read poetry or has never read poetry. Yet, once they hear poetry or read it, they find they like it. It's been my experience in the classroom, whether I'm working in Writers-in-the-Schools with a class of sixth graders, or in a college classroom, that people have great hang-ups about poetry. But once they read it, once they find out what it is, once they find out that they didn't like it for the wrong reasons, they didn't like it because they thought they shouldn't like it, certain barriers come down. That, I think, is related to my sense of an audience. My sources in my writing are my experiences, my dreams, certainly the larger questions of facing death, living in a particular place, and how that place may or may not be like any other place, questions of political realities all around us, questions of gender, and so on. I guess that's a long answer to the question of audience, but it's a tremendously important question to me. It goes down to my root definition of what being a writer is, and it goes back to what we talked about quite a while ago. That is, the idea of *seeing* and having a kind of vision that you want to share that's more than a private vision, that touches on something that you hope will stir something deep in your reader as it has stirred something deep within yourself.

A VINZ POETRY SAMPLER:
1972-1987

In The Heartland

Who can say
why the birds in this country
crash so hopelessly against
the windows of passing cars?
The ditches by the highway
are filled with their broken wings—
the intestines of rotting rabbits,
raccoon fur, a calf trying to rise
from the pulpy mound
that used to be his hindquarters,
three dogs, one without a head,
a cat hanging from a thin wire noose
on a dead elm tree branch...

All along the main streets
tv sets are turning off.
The houses look like old men
squatting in long rows,
ready to pitch forward into the earth
as easily as pebbles slipping into still water.

1972

65

Winter Promises

The funeral procession
creeps out from behind the church,
a long black snake filled with
the faces of captive children
and fingers drawing backward
messages on the steamed glass.

But what do they do with the bodies
when it's 25 below,
when the ground's as hard
as this ice-ridden road,
deep down
deeper than any grave
impossible to dig?

I dream of them
stacked like cordwood
in some refrigerated vault,
waiting for spring thaw,
the mansions of heaven
temporarily delayed.

I dream of them
in the dark cellars of the prairie,
frozen with the potatoes, with doors
and rocks and tent poles, with
broken pots and buffalo meat.

And here above ground:
the frosty halos of our breath,
the driven snow
that flies in through our eyes.

1972

I. Dear Sir:

I am a confessional poet
from Decatur, Illinois.
My mother is a librarian,
my father sells used cars.
My poems, as you will see,
are mostly about snakes
and sunsets.

After all,
how much is there to confess
in Decatur, Illinois?

1974

II. to whom it may concern:

No one knows how a poet suffers.
These are some of my poems.
They are about suffering.
I have collected nearly 3,000
rejection slips in the last 5 years.

Please send me one of yours.

1974

IX. Editor:

Over a week ago, I sent you
15 poems. As yet I have not
received your reply.
Kindly take what you like
and send the rest directly on
to *Denver Quarterly*.

It's already August, and I'm
still not through the D's.

1974

Red River Blues

Tonight the news of drought
sweeps in on western winds—
topsoil laced with smoke and snow.
Nothing can stop that message here.

The empty rain gauge chants
the last faint summer dreams;
around the house the earth
has sunk another inch this week.

Even flat land falls away: this is
the place where all directions cease.
Just past town is the only hill—
the overpass for the Interstate.

1976

Growing Season
—for Betsy

Does it matter that your garden's
ripe with weeds—the first
you've ever helped to grow?
Amazement is your major crop:
those seeds did sprout, and now
the thick cucumber vines hide flowers.
The corn is higher than your waist—
slender leaves have made a fence
that holds you more than most.

This year you'll let the others make
pilgrimage to mountains or the coasts.
Flat land has become enough—
perhaps you're simply growing old.

A chilly midnight winds calls you out
to watch the elms along the boulevard—
each a dark thunderhead, speaking
tongues you know. The grass
is damp from where the children
turned the sprinkler on. They danced.
You sang—of gardens, seeds, and snow.

1976

Alma Mater

The hallways are a map
I still can read,
legend printed
just above the front door.
One inch equals 20 years.

They have moved the office,
changed the names and doors,
reset the colors and the clocks.
Only the faces are familiar:
all who enter here
still need a pass.

Tell us,
what shrinks?
Everything.

Tell us.
what shrinks?
Only me.

1975

Tourist Class: A Triptych

Greyhound

There are only two of you now.
The old man across the aisle
has been coughing for weeks
beneath the last good light.
One day you must speak to him
about all this dirt and litter.

Outside, the small towns
flash their lights into your eyes
and disappear forever.
There are no masters here,
and no survivors.

Diner

Two booths down
a man keeps waving at the mirrors—
smiles, then shields his face
and weeps into his fries.

The hooker lets you know
she's waited over 30 years
to settle down.
Her gentleman smiles toothlessly
and plunges toward her knees.

You watch the waitress navigate her aisles,
coffee rising on the walls.
You watch the old campaigner at the counter
eye No Loitering signs
waiting for a flock of pigeons to feed.

When the country music plays
everyone whistles in a different key.
No refunds here.
Nobody is allowed to leave.

Motel

Don't be misled by
swimming pools or aisles.
Each room here is vacant,
each a kind of small museum.
It may take years
to find the right one.
You will know it by the way
the doorknob matches your pulse.
When you enter, there will be
no need to turn on the light.

1975

Libra

Your horoscope advises peace-making,
what you were born to do.
Diplomat of coffee stain and broken hinge,
you praise the falling leaves,
the coils of dust beneath your bed,
the old dog circling one last time before
she finds her place beneath your flickering lamp.
Late September moon ascending,
orange and full and wet. Mantra of worn clocks.
Empty school rooms slumber in the dark,
swollen eyes at the window.
What is it you have learned?
That you have traveled far enough
to start the journey back.
That your promises rise and fall
with weather, seasons, tides.
That the slender hammock of your sleep
is strung between two doors:
      what you'll fail to do tomorrow,
      what you've failed to do today.

1977

Contingency Plan

Ground zero is
a leaky water pipe,
your desk piled deep
with promises,
caverns beneath your eyes.

For a moment
the phone stops ringing.

Children
fed and washed
by your own hand
lie singing in their beds.

Snowflakes drift in
between window cracks,
billowing the curtains
into a sail.

1975

Survival Manual

Flat land has its own beauty too.
I've listened to a horde of folks
just passing through—
all they seem to see is dust and clouds.
They wouldn't know alfalfa from oats,
a Holstein from an antelope.
Sure, a few of them stop to take
a snapshot of a quaint, dilapidated barn,
or the old steam thresher abandoned
in the tall grass behind the Cenex station.
For a while I even took to posing in my braces
and seed hat in front of the pool hall—
when there was a pool hall, and not
that damned quarter-sized, quarter-eating
table in the back corner of the Sportsman Bar.

I got a kick out of that—
even sold some little plastic ashtrays
with *Deep Water* embossed in fake gold leaf
(13 bucks a gross from some Florida mail order
house; I found the ad in the Minneapolis *Star*).

Familiar ground—I know, I've covered it all.
Whatever it is that holds us here
is some part love and some part hate,
but it helps to have a little laughter too,
and stubbornness.

1978

Old Doc

His gimpy leg was testimony to
some other surgeon's art—
he was the best, though he'd never
tell you that.

He drove a big green Oldsmobile
until his hands started shaking—
there were some folks who could
never forgive him that—
not the car, the hands,
the drinks he'd take each day
down at the Sportsman Bar
just to pass the time between
the mailbox and his empty office
over the grocery store.
What these folks forget could fill
an elevator bin—
the horse and buggy days,
the times he sweated through a blizzard
to deliver a baby on a failing farm
somewhere so far out in the sticks
you'd need a compass and a prayer to find it.
With spring thaw those farmers
brought him sacks of potatoes from
their cellar holes, and jars of
pickled beets and corn.
Money? Hell, there wasn't any left,
but he stayed on, and when the
Valley City clinic started up
the town folks left him for it,
just like flies to a new corpse.

Sure, he was the best.
And now there's not a doctor living
within 30 miles of here—
nor was there when *his* stroke came around.

1978

Discount Shopping
—for Jim Stevens

We never see each other
outside these barn-like walls—
the fat madonnas cradling
babies, blouses, plastic boots,
the husbands wheeling loads of
ties and motor oil.
Today the uniform is bulging
orlon tops and papery double knits.
A herd of pimples rummages
the 8-track tapes, old campaigners
form a skirmish line of canes,
checkout artists pop their gum at 90 r.p.m.
Ever wonder why the faces never change?

Beneath this store and parking lot
a secret city sprawls—
it's where the workers go after hours
to reproduce the merchandise
and engineer the sales.
Most of the shippers live there too—
study muzak, elbowing, and cartsmanship—
come up to browse on 8 hour shifts.

Now and then a few defect:
they disappear for weeks, then overnight
put up bungalows at the edge of town.

1976

81

Business As Usual

Under the dining room light
the old conspiracy flickers:
who failed the checkbook this time,
who hid the newspaper, tipped the ashtray,
left windows open in the rain...

The children are upstairs in bed
listening to the grass growing—
it's simple now, in moonlight.
All day they have been speaking to
Mr. South Wind, asking favors:
blow away the neighbors
in their lawnchairs, bring
some new friends in a balloon.

But fathers are useful, too.
I'm required to teach them how to spell
so they can write their dreams,
required to learn a magic chant
to make tornadoes go away,
to tame a big bull cat for them,
and watch their hands, and sing.

And since I cannot fix the tv set
or the ugly eye of a ceiling leak,
cannot make the insects stop
squashing themselves against the screens,
since I am not on speaking terms with
the south wind, or the cupboard crickets,
or even the column of figures
I helped to invent.

It's really the least I can do

here beside the window
and a whole army of healthy grass
growing greener
growing loud
in the last lovely light
of the moon, the moon, the moon.

1974   82

A Harvest

It is autumn, when the geese
chime midnight just above your roof,
when you remember nearly everything
you couldn't live without
all these years—
perhaps what keeps you sleepless
on the nights you'd least expect
betrayal from your oldest friends—
the moon, a few certain stars and sounds,
shadows from the elm trees
just inside the deepest dark.
You wait, not yet old
but more unsure each day.

Tonight is autumn and the geese have gone.
God, like some grandfather who has died too soon,
perhaps is laughing softly now
at all your metaphors—
just as you laugh your tiredest, shuddering self
backward through the lengthening nights.
But the child upon the stairs is sleepless too,
wakened by a speeding car with music
that some nerve inside you hates.
Together you will listen to the leaves—
whatever drops away, whatever stays.

1977

The Queen Game

The children gather round the television set for the Miss America pageant—
the Queen Game, as they call it. Who will gain the crown tonight, who will
hold the winning ticket in the great dream lottery? This is the spectacle they
love the best, better even than the Academy Awards or the telethon for crip-
pled children.

Miss Arkansas gets two votes out of three. She sings off key a song from
Oklahoma, but her hair is auburn and her mouth is full of perfect teeth. The
emcee croons his spiel again, Miss California twirls a hula-hoop, Wyoming
prances on a trampoline. Even the children know that talent doesn't matter
here. It's all in the smile, isn't it? They watch, transfixed: Rapunzel and her
golden hair, the Cinderella gown, the miller's daughter who will charm a
king. And just beyond the lights and screen the cruel stepmothers gather and
clap their withered hands.

1979

Angler

He hadn't been at it very long when he discovered that he was becoming addicted to something. It wasn't the fish, which he didn't like to handle or eat, and it wasn't the company of other fishermen, which he disliked even more. He simply had to go, and the fact that he'd never learned to swim and was still terribly afraid of drowning did not stop him from heading into deeper and deeper water each time, even though he knew there were few fish in water of that depth. For one reason or another he filed the sharp barbs off his hooks, and sometimes he even forgot to put on the bait.

He knew that someday he would use up all his line, and the thought bothered him from time to time. But still he fished on alone, deeper and deeper into the dark green shadows, for he also knew that no matter how much line he let out, he would never reach bottom.

1979

85

Holes In His Underwear

For God's sake, his mother always told him, never go out with holes in your underwear. What if you were in an accident? She was a good and dutiful mother and could be proud that he was always equipped with the best Fruit of the Loom—spotless, bleached, and even starched.

But then he went off to college and began to forget everything she had labored so long to teach him, and one day he was in a terrible car wreck. When the surgeons gathered in the Emergency Room they were amazed to find that not only was his underwear in shreds, he hadn't washed behind his ears or brushed his teeth in weeks. This would be a case for the medical journals. His poor mother was bereft. How could she face the rest of her life with the knowledge she'd failed so miserably? It was all right there in the AP press release: her name, the mother whose son was in an accident with holes in his underwear.

1979

The Weird Kid

Charlie was the weird kid—there's always one in every class, and even if I've forgotten his last name, I haven't forgotten that it was in fifth grade with a teacher none of us liked very much. And I still remember him every time I see a ball-point smudge, for Charlie was one long streak of smeared ink. He seemed to ooze ink, and cowlicks, and ripped seams, and tardy slips. He was the suicidal one who perfected the head-first slide in baseball—on a gravel playground. He was the kid whose homework was never done, who always smelled funny and had fuzzy teeth, who tracked in mud from the schoolyard and got sent back to clean his shoes three or four times till he got it right.

Charlie was the only kid I ever knew who dared to let farts during the flag salute. He was the only kid who was crazy enough to dip Mary Kay's braids in an ink bottle; she was the one beautiful girl in the fifth grade, and Charlie must have known that five or six of the hulking types would be waiting for him after school to pulverize him for Mary Kay's honor and their pleasure. And it was Charlie who told me my first really filthy joke—in fact, he told the whole class, one day when the teacher decided to indulge us all with a new kind of fun called "Joke Sharing Hour," which, thanks to Charlie lasted only about five minutes and was never held again, not even on the best of days.

And long after all the beautiful Mary Kays were married off and manufacturing beautiful children, long after the Wallys and Steves had packed away their baseball gear forever, long after the Geralds and Dianas had won full scholarships to the graduate schools of their choice, Charlie is the one I still wonder about. He's probably a bartender or a race car driver or a deck hand—whatever it is, he's not very good at it, still sweating out a lifetime of principal's offices. But I wish I had him here right now—maybe to thank him, to tell him that even if all of us were embarrassed about him and really didn't like him very much, he was a kind of martyr we could always count on to take the heat off everyone else. I'd at least like to show him what I've written about him, to show him the way I still smudge my own ink, and tell him that sometimes now I'm even able to admit it.

1980

87

Father To Father

Children, Father—
how strange each day
to see more of you in me,
more of me in them.
This is one game for which
you never taught me rules,
and now as I begin to feel my age
move in me like lodestone
perhaps we have something
to talk out after all—
two old men unsure
of where it really starts or ends.

I sit up late
scratching something out
while all my darlings sleep,
and curse the noisy neighbor
or the barking dogs—
that never wake them anyway.
This seems to be my job,
to play their night
like some shadowy Orpheus—
I, who can remember only the dark,
a father 30 years ago at a kitchen table
moving toward first light
with bread, milk, and *Reader's Digest*.
What was it *you* heard—
you, who understand
neither sons nor poems?

Perhaps this same thing I pass on,
so one day all that's given
is returned.
Love? Duty? Fear? Hard words
for men who speak so sparingly.
Tonight it's time to say it, Father,
what's taken all these years:
I have daughters, you have a son.
Only the name ends here.

Meditations On A Green Apple

for Bill Holm:
"Even little things delight us;
For these little things we yearn."

I.

It waits on the kitchen counter,
inscrutable green intruder
in a basket of red delicious.
"How can you eat that sour thing?"
I'm asked, feeling my lips pucker
at the mere suggestion.

II.

Of a late summer afternoon
the backyard trees sagged with them.
How we loved their forbidden greenness—
even the tiny crabs, better for
throwing than for eating—
gangs of apple-stealing boys
who carried salt shakers in their pockets,
scuttling through fences, hedges, minefields,
laying schemes in dark garages,
eating, eating, eating their way
toward bellyache and dreams of
apple-guarding dogs and
angry citizens with rakes.

III.

Our own lone tree was safe—
never producing more than a
dozen or so apples, those in the
highest branches where my father
and I tried to knock them into
coffee cans tied to long cane poles—
a pie or two a year, no more,
yet round that tree each night
mounds of green apple cores
and the brave tales of apple raiders.

IV.

Old man shaking his fist,
goes muttering in to his wife
about what the world is coming to.
"Boys," she says, stirring
raw egg into fresh ground coffee,
"or have you forgotten?"

Blessed be all old men who
shake their fists at apple-stealing boys.
Perhaps they came to know how much
we needed them,
how much they needed us.

V.

Tart and green
the apple waits on the counter—
supermarket safe, too sweet, perhaps,
too quiet—and outside the window
no apple trees and no boys.

Alone in a winter kitchen
a man bites into a green apple—
lets the juice run down his chin.

1985

Mac

"Good Egg"—her favorite words
for those she liked—beyond that,
all was Irish flare and curse.
She had a temper made for feuds
and kept her whiskey in the fridge
so she wouldn't have to fool with ice.
And when they cut her open just to find
they couldn't stop the cancer,
she went back to the nursing home
from which she'd just retired
as head night nurse—
helpless, hairless, strangely mute.
And if they ever stopped to watch
the terrible irony at work
they never seemed to show it—
condescending, starched, and vague.
Old women die of cancer every day,
even the tough and lonely ones
stripped of all but the crying out.
Was she patient here or nurse?

She used to tell stories of the ones
whose age had finally snapped—
night walkers, shriekers, babblers,
old men running naked in the halls.
I never heard her speak
of those who only had to wait,
nor the hands that must have reached out.
But then, this page is cold
with all that I've forgotten,
my last and only Irish aunt:
Good night, Old Dear, "Good Egg."

1981

91

At the Funeral of the Poets
for Alec Bond, 1938-1985

It would be an old house, I think,
somewhere past the edge of town—
40 good acres of oak and pine,
a little river with a boat for fishing
and deer to come and drink in waning light.
There would have to be birds
so we could learn the names and sounds again,
perhaps a pasture with a horse or two,
rooms with books and photographs
and crocks of homemade beer.

When the screen door creaks you'll know
they're going to call us in to eat—
roasted corn and ribs, three kinds of bread
thick sliced and warm, and soup so rich
you'll wonder where you've never lived
to taste such soup as this—and then the wine,
and all night long to sit on front porch swings
or stroll around the yard
listening to each voice from shadows—
quick small breezes bearing
scents of flowers and faroff ripening fields,
and lights in upstairs rooms that burn into the dawn.

1985

Shooting Signs

Just once I'd like to drive
a stretch in northern Minnesota
and find road signs with
no bullet holes in them.
I've never met anyone who
admitted to shooting signs—
abandoned farmhouses are
another matter, though I've heard
it's mostly kids with shotguns
getting back at their parents
for all those years of table manners—
the same way, my friend Keith
tells me, loud tailpipes are a
teenager's means of farting in public.
But who shoots all those signs?
Someone no doubt has written
a book on the subject, and
here's another chapter for him:
let's fill the woods with signs—
stop signs, yield signs, curve signs,
Men Working signs, and of course
the ones with leaping deer.
Then, let all those hunters go
out to the woods and shoot their fill—
signs or each other, nothing else.
Think of all the people we could
employ making signs, designing signs,
managing and maintaining signs!
Think of you and me on a hot afternoon
at the office—we just grab our 30-30's
and jump in the pickup truck, head out
to the woods for some shooting, old pard,
for some serious fun, you bet!

1986

Finding the Big Ones

> "All poems are love poems"
> —Raymond Carver

The local oracle tilts back his brew—
You've got to know the lake, he says.
The big bass are in the cabbage weed
and thick coontail—use sucker minnows,
the fat ones; forget that plastic crap.

The room is full of nods, our best
aficionado smiles—which also say
we know already nothing much will happen,
that it's always something more
than the right place, the right bait.
And back in the car we'll have to
speculate again just what went wrong
this time. Fishermen, so full of love
we hardly remember the way home.

1984

Homesteaders

I.

When they came
some of them already knew
that here was more than flatness;
here at last was a place
where all things would be possible.

II.

Call it ocean, call it desert;
trails move off in all directions—
tall grass, wheatfield, open range.
Everyone here is traveler.
No one knows the way.

III.

The buffalo wallow is thick with prairie aster,
coneflower, gentian, blazing star.
We walk the fields till dusk,
when deer come down to drink at the river
and a cool wind ruffles the bluestem.
The sky is full of old bones.

1984

Celebrity Seal Found Dead

That's what the headline from the AP wire story says, but someone has cut out the rest of the page, so there's no story. But what's there to tell, really? It's all too familiar by now—another victim of controlled substances, fishy binges in New York and LA, the same tired screed of slippery accusations. He worked for smallfry when he should have ruled the tank, and then one day even Dave and Johnny stopped calling. They claimed he just didn't give a toot anymore. *Enquirer* claimed he'd been seen with sharks in dives. *He* claimed he was cleaning up his act, learning some new tunes, barking up another tree— so what if his career was on the rocks, he'd resurface soon... That's when they found him, whisker-down in the pool. You can imagine the rest—small wake, sealed coffin, the mysterious porpoise in black. It's all too familiar.

So watch for the book and made-for-TV movie out this fall. And remember this: a lot of us mammals love the clapping too much for our own good. Who can really blame his getting tired of shelling out? Face it, he was a showman—right to the salty end, all the way to the unfathomable bottom.

1987

97

The Man Who Holds the Camera

In the photograph, I'm the one who keeps his head down, showing teeth. It's hard to smile when you're squinting into sun. It's hard to look excited after riding for hours in the back seat, watching the tops of trees. But this is the country and we're having fun. Smile, my father says in double-breasted gabardine and felt hat shadowing his eyes—the hat I play with when he's not looking, when I drive my pot-lid car in the kitchen, to New York or to India, never to the country in the flat, still light of Sunday afternoon. Smile for the camera, my father says—he's not in many pictures. I noticed even then. The faces pale, my mother's red dress slips to rusty brown, all else to shades of gray. We're in the country, having fun on Sunday afternoon—squinting at the man who holds the camera, trying hard to smile.

1987

Sleeping Till Noon

Upstairs, my daughter lies swaddled in her bedsheets like an Eastern princess. Good sleeping weather last night—any summer night is good for her. Lawn-mowers, barking dogs, phone calls, the man next door scraping paint to raucous music—none of it matters to her, and I won't wake her either, not for anything less than the Second Coming. Not till noon, anyway. That's when my father's voice takes over. I can't help it. When I grew up, certain things were always held sacred—long distance calls, cleaning your plate, getting up at a "decent" hour.

But let's face it—I don't sleep so well anymore, no matter what my intentions. Sunlight shakes me like there's something urgent I've forgotten. Alarm clocks follow me into every room.

So sleep well, daughter, sleep well for both of us on this fine summer morning. I'll take the phone off the hook, go outside and speak to birds and garbage trucks, and when we meet on the stairs it will be with guilty smiles. Here's one thing, at least, I haven't managed to forget. Good morning, daughter. And yes, indeed, it was.

1987

99

ACKNOWLEDGEMENTS

Collections and First Publications if Other Than the Collection

from *Winter Promises*:

"In the Heartland"   *The Lamp in the Spine*, 4 (Spring 1972)
"Winter Promises"

from *Letters to the Poetry Editor*:

Poems numbered I, II, IX, XX, and XXI

from *Red River Blues*:

"Red River Blues" (also in *Minnesota Gothic*)
"Growing Season" *Studio One* (Spring 1977) (also in *Mixed Blessings*)

from *Songs for A Hometown Boy*:

"Alma Mater" *Moons and Lion Tailes*, 4 (January 1976)
"Tourist Class" *Crazy Horse*, 17 (Summer 1977)

from *Contingency Plans*:

"Contingency Plans" (also in *Mixed Blessings*)
"Libra" (also in *Mixed Blessings*)
"Processional" (also in *Mixed Blessings*)

from *Deep Water, Dakota*:

"Survival Manual"
"Old Doc" *Dakota Arts Quarterly*, 7 (1979)

from *Climbing the Stairs*:

"Business As Usual" *North American Review* (Summer 1976)
"Discount Shopping" *Pendragon* (Summer 1984)
"A Harvest" *Georgia Review* (Fall 1979)

from *The Weird Kid*:

"Angler"
"The Queen Game"
"Holes in His Underwear"
"The Weird Kid" *Poetry Now*, 6, 6 (1982)

from *Mixed Blessings*:

"Meditations on A Green Apple" *Minnesota Monthly* (December 1986)
"Mac" *Northeast* (Winter 1981-82)
"Father to Father" *North American Review* (June 1981)
"At the Funeral of the Poets" *Minnesota Monthly* (September 1986)
"North of North" *South Dakota Review* (Autumn 1983)

from *Minnesota Gothic*:

"Shooting Signs"
"Finding the Big Ones" *Northern Review* (1987)
"Homesteaders" *North Dakota Quarterly* (Fall 1985)

from *Late Night Calls*:

"Celebrity Seal Found Dead"
"The Man Who Holds the Camera"
"Sleeping Till Noon" *The Spoon River Quarterly* (Spring 1987)

+ "Processional," "North of North," and *Letters* XX and XXI are from the interview

Photo credits: for the photo on page iv, thanks to J. Naiden, Compas; on page 2 to Wayne Gudmundson; on page 12 to Thom Tammaro; on page 14 to Mark Vinz; on page 24 to Mark Vinz; on page 39 to Wayne Gudmundson; on page 62 to Mark Vinz; on page 64 to Mark Vinz; on page 70 to Carol Alexander; on page 92 (top) to Mark Vinz and (bottom) Joe Richardson; on page 100 to Thom Tammaro.